A KING IN HIDING

HOW A CHILD REFUGEE BECAME A WORLD CHESS CHAMPION

FAHIM

WITH SOPHIE LE CALLENNEC AND XAVIER PARMENTIER

TRANSLATED FROM THE FRENCH BY BARBARA MELLOR

ICON

Published in the UK in 2015 by
Icon Books Ltd, Omnibus Business Centre,
39–41 North Road, London N7 9DP
email: info@iconbooks.com
www.iconbooks.com

Sold in the UK, Europe and Asia
by Faber & Faber Ltd, Bloomsbury House,
74–77 Great Russell Street,
London WC1B 3DA or their agents

Distributed in the UK, Europe and Asia
by TBS Ltd, TBS Distribution Centre, Colchester Road,
Frating Green, Colchester CO7 7DW

Distributed to the trade in the USA
by Consortium Book Sales and Distribution
The Keg House, 34 Thirteenth Avenue NE,
Suite 101, Minneapolis, MN 55413-1007

Distributed in Australia and New Zealand
by Allen & Unwin Pty Ltd, PO Box 8500,
83 Alexander Street, Crows Nest, NSW 2065

Distributed in South Africa by
Jonathan Ball, Office B4, The District,
41 Sir Lowry Road, Woodstock 7925

Distributed in Canada by Publishers Group Canada,
76 Stafford Street, Unit 300
Toronto, Ontario M6J 2S1

ISBN: 978-184831-828-1

Typeset in Adobe Text Pro by Marie Doherty

Printed and bound in the UK by Clays Ltd, St Ives plc

CONTENTS

ABOUT THE AUTHORS

Fahim was born in Bangladesh. At the age of eight, he had to flee with his father to escape a threat of abduction. They journeyed across Asia and Europe and eventually settled in France. While they struggled to make a life for themselves as illegal immigrants, Fahim, already a keen chess player, was talent-spotted by Xavier Parmentier, who took him under his wing and trained him for competition. In 2012, Fahim won the French national Junior Chess Championship. In 2013, he won the World School Chess Championship Under-13 title.

Sophie Le Callennec is an anthropologist and expert in East African geography, and has written numerous school textbooks. She taught French to Fahim's father, and lent her pen to their story.

Xavier Parmentier is a Master of the International Chess Federation (FIDE) and a renowned professional coach in France. He has coached the national junior chess team for twenty years. He is currently Director of Training for professional coaches within the French Chess Federation. He is personally involved as a volunteer coach for young talent in chess clubs in the Paris suburbs.

Barbara Mellor has 30 years' experience as a translator and editor, specialising in art, architecture, history, fashion and design; her translation of Agnès Humbert's wartime journal, *Résistance: Memoirs of Occupied France* (Bloomsbury, 2008) received widespread praise.

PROLOGUE

On 4 May 2012, two days before the second round of the French presidential elections, prime minister François Fillon was the guest on the phone-in segment of the *France Inter* morning radio show. A caller rang in to raise the case of a young boy of eleven who had just been crowned French national chess champion. The boy was a homeless asylum seeker whose appeal had been refused, who was living in hiding with his father in the Paris suburb of Créteil, in constant fear of deportation. The affair had attracted media attention over recent days, and it had caused a considerable stir. In response, François Fillon promised live on air that he would look into the boy's case. Within a few days it had been settled.

The boy's name was Fahim. At the point when his story started to attract attention, I was living in Créteil. I knew his father, as I had been part of the support network that had grown up around them. I had known Xavier, his chess master, for ever. When it came to writing their story, it seemed natural for them to turn to me: to listen to Fahim, to express his thoughts, interpret his silences and be at his side throughout the writing process.

I could not have imagined how close we would become over those months spent together. How often Fahim would come to my house, where I live with my children. How in addition to telling the story of his past, he would also ask for my help in building his future.

This is the story of a small boy who used to live in a distant land, a good little boy who was loved, and who – like all children of his age – spent his days playing and daydreaming. Until the world of grown-ups decided otherwise.

This is the heartbreaking story of how, at the age of just eight, he was forced to leave all this and to flee his country, to seek refuge far away from his home and his loved ones. Of how his world damaged and destroyed him until he managed to snatch the right to live a normal life. It is also the story of how he encountered a remarkable man. It is a tale of modern life from which – largely thanks to this man – hope and solidarity emerge triumphant.

I have written this book with Fahim. The words and feelings are his. I give them to you. And I give them back to him.

Sophie Le Callennec

For my father

For everyone who has helped me and everyone who continues to help me

Fahim

Chapter 1

THE CHESS PLAYER

My father was good. Very good. He was always play-ing chess and he always won. At home he played for hours. Several times a week he went to the chess club and stayed there late into the night.

There were chess sets everywhere in our house. Boards of all sizes, pieces in all shapes, and books on chess. A world in black and white. When my father played chess with his friends, I would sit and watch: I said nothing, understood nothing. Afterwards, I would race outside to play with my friends.

One day when I was five, my father said:

'Would you like to come to the club with me?'

He'd never taken me with him before. I was a bit wor-ried that it would be boring, but I said yes. I was proud. We crossed Dhaka to reach an impressive building in the banking district. At the end of a long passage lined by men smoking and talking, we came to a big room full of people. Everyone knew my father and said hello to him, then they asked my name or if I would like a drink.

When they started to play, the atmosphere became serious and the heat pressed down. The players made their moves at top speed. They tapped on the clocks beside them and made all sorts of other clicking and rapping noises. I could hear little yelps, sometimes of surprise, sometimes of joy or despair. It was all very different from the quiet way my father played at home. To begin with it was fun to watch, but soon I got bored. I didn't dare to disturb my father, so I sat on a chair, swinging my legs, and waited.

A man came up to me:

'Would you like me to teach you?'

I didn't dare disappoint him.

'Yes …', I whispered.

He went off to fetch a large wooden board, put pieces on it one by one, according to some mysterious rule, and started to explain. I listened, but it was complicated. So I said nothing and stifled my yawns so as not to be rude.

Back at home, I thought about chess. The thoughts went round and round in my head and got all muddled up, but I wanted to understand it. I asked my father about it, and he was surprised: it was obvious to him that the game didn't interest me. But I wouldn't give up, so he set up a chessboard on the low table in the living room and I tried to memorise where the pieces went. He introduced them to me:

'This one with the cross, is the "king", and this one with the crown is the "queen". These are the "rooks", "knights" and "bishops".'

'Why do they have English names?'

'Because the British colonised Bangladesh and taught us how to play in their language.'

They looked funny and made me laugh.

The next day I tackled him again:

'*Abba* [Dad in Bengali], what do the rooks do?'

My father explained, showing me how the pieces move and teaching me how you capture your opponent's. Between the king who moves one square at a time, the queen who can cross the board in one go and the pawns who move forward one or sometimes two squares but take other pieces diagonally, it was really complicated. But exciting. So I asked more questions, the next day and the day after. More and more, over and over.

'*Abba*, how do the knights move?'

'*Abba*, how does the king capture other pieces?'

'*Abba*, which is stronger, a rook or a bishop?'

Patiently, my father would explain it all to me, putting me right and encouraging me. Then after a while he would stop with a sigh and promise me:

'Tomorrow we'll see if you've got it clearer in your head.'

The next day we would start again. My father would teach me how to defend my pieces, show me how to scare my opponent. I loved chess, but inside my head it was all a muddle. I made stupid moves. I was no good.

My father knew it. He must have done. Because every time he ended up heaving a sigh and stopping:

'OK, Fahim, we'll carry on tomorrow.'

Maybe chess was just too difficult for me. Maybe I was the worst chess player in the world. Too bad! I carried on. I wanted to understand. I was determined to get better, however long it took.

One day, my father showed me a trick for surprising my opponent and trapping his king. All of a sudden, the chessboard came to life: the pieces jumped up and stood in rows, the rooks headed straight for the enemy camp, the bishops zoomed to and fro, the knights leaped about all over the place, the pawns obeyed unquestioningly, even when their orders meant risking their own lives in order to free a senior officer who'd been taken prisoner by the enemy; the king, weak, slow and almost insignificant, was as docile as a baby, and begged me to save him from death; and the queen, my queen, strong, quick and clever, pirouetted around the board, dominating the fight.

It wasn't a chess match any more, it was a battle. It wasn't a game, it was war. I mustered my troops, sent out messengers, set traps, decided who to keep and who to sacrifice, protected them and led them to victory.

It was a week since I'd started to learn, and now I understood: I could play!

Chapter 2

LIFE WAS GOOD

XAVIER PARMENTIER: *I'm a chess master. I've taught chess for over 30 years now. Before I met Fahim and he became my pupil, I could locate Bangladesh on a globe, sharing a border with India. I knew it was one of the world's poorest countries, but I wouldn't have been able to tell you that its capital was Dhaka. And I didn't know either that it is so much at the mercy of typhoons, cyclones, tsunamis and floods that by the end of the century, unless we do something to halt climate change, it will be swallowed up by the oceans.*

It was when I began to take an interest in Fahim that I started to really find out about this country where he was born and spent the first eight years of his life: a country smaller than Tunisia with a population larger than Russia, where one child in five suffers from malnutrition even before they are born. And before this little guy turned up at the club that I ran, I would certainly never have associated Bangladesh with the world of chess. It didn't take me long to realise that Fahim was very different from our usual image of immigrants from developing countries. He didn't live in a shanty town in Dhaka, and he wasn't a street kid, roaming the dusty highways and dodging cars and cycle rickshaws to beg a few coins from passers by who didn't care. He hadn't left his country to flee poverty. Quite the reverse, in fact: he came from a middle-class family who, without being exactly wealthy, nevertheless lived a life that was tranquil and free of troubles.

My father was a fireman: he saved people's lives. When there was an accident, he used to go off in the red truck with the siren blaring. When there was a fire, he would put it out. When someone was drowning, he would dive into the river to save them.

In the evening, he used to tell us stories about the people whose lives he'd saved, the tragedies he'd prevented. And then there were the times when he couldn't help, like the story about the man who woke up in the middle of the night to find his house was on fire, and who was so poor that his first thought was to save the only thing he owned, his television. When he went back in to save his sons, it was already too late: the building had gone up in flames, with his children imprisoned inside. He stood there watching. He howled and wailed. Then he picked up his television and hurled it into the flames. My father also told us how his commanding officer had sacked him from the ambulance team because he'd refused to demand money from a very poor woman who had to be rushed to hospital because she was having a baby.

Then my father got old: he was over 40 and he retired from his job. He didn't save people's lives any more, but he went to the barracks every day because we lived nearby, because he was friends with the firemen, and because he liked looking after the garden there. And he had a new job: he set up a car hire company. The rest of the time he played chess. He and a friend started a chess club. People poked fun at first, but then they stopped: it was a very good club and it became famous.

We were rich. We lived in a big house with two rooms: a bedroom with a double bed for me and my sister, and the living room, which had my parents' bed in the corner. And the baby's bed too.

It was a lovely house, but it needed a lot of repairs. One day, a great chunk of ceiling came down right beside me and scared the life out of me. Cyclones were frightening too: it felt as though the wind was going to tear the walls apart. It wasn't just me who got worried either: our neighbours would come to our house and say prayers in Arabic. The monsoon season didn't bother me though. The rains were torrential, there was water everywhere and everyone got fed up with it, but it wasn't frightening. When the courtyard turned into a lake, the neighbours would pile up sandbags so they could walk about without getting their feet wet. Sometimes the water would come up over the steps and into the house.

I knew we were rich because my father was the only one in our family – in our whole neighbourhood – to buy a cow for Eid: everyone else just had sheep or chickens. I would lead the cow home and my father and a friend would cut its throat. The blood would spurt all over the place, but I was used to it. What I didn't like was the look in the cow's eyes as it died: I could see it was afraid. Would it be the same for a person, I used to wonder?

On the day of the feast, my mother and father would prepare food for everybody: family, neighbours and firemen. My mother's cooking was so good that everyone wanted to come and share with us. So she would spread the floor with big cloths of all colours for our guests to sit on. Then we could dig in. What a spread!

I liked everything about my life. Except for school. In the morning my parents would shake me awake, gently at first, then more roughly. In the end I would get up, but I was always in a bad mood. I wouldn't speak until I got to school. As soon as I was back with my friends again I would feel better.

I spent my first year in a school where the lessons were too easy. I was always top of the class. So my parents sent me to a private school that was very expensive.

I was a good pupil and did as I was told. I didn't have much choice. In Bangladesh the teachers were strict: if you didn't work, they hit you with a stick. There were 70 of us in my class, and we all took turns to get beaten. Or all the boys did, anyway: the girls used to work hard and never got beaten. One day the teacher hit a boy so hard that he had to stay at home for a week while his wounds healed.

Like all the others, I went to school in the morning and studied with tutors in the afternoon. Some of the children in my class cheated, and had private lessons with teachers from the school, so that they would know what to revise for the tests. The tutors my sister and I had didn't know which topics were going to come up, so they would make us do our homework and then give us more. When it was time to pray, I would sometimes tell them I had to go to prayers and then run off and play with my friends.

There was a shared courtyard in front of our house where we used to play cricket, and sometimes badminton. There was a big tree with branches that got in the way, but no one could remember who it belonged to: the neighbours argued about who planted it, and unless they could agree no one could cut it back. When we got fed up with the tree, my friends and I would go off to find other places to play. When I was little, we used to go

12

swimming in the lake. But then it got all dirty and over-grown, with snakes lurking in the tall grass, so we stayed away, even when the heat was suffocating. We would roam around to other places, along the path behind the firemen's barracks or in front of the mosque. One time, our parents came out looking for us everywhere. When he found me my father was furious, with big black angry eyes. He told me I had to stay either in the courtyard or at the barracks.

Sometimes my mother and sister used to take me to the cinema. We would queue up to get in and it was always jam-packed. The films were always love stories (with a little dance) with a happy ending (and a little dance). Even when the hero died, he would come back for the finale (and a little dance). I liked animations better.

My sister was four years older than me. Her name was Jhorna, which means 'waterfall'. I was always argu-ing with her, which used to make our parents cross:

'Dad gave that money to *me* to buy a snack.'

'No! He said we had to share it.'

'That's not true! He said I could spend it on what I wanted!'

Every morning it was a race for the bathroom:

'*I'm* going to have my shower.'

'No, I said *I'm* going first.'

'Too late!'

If I complained to my mother, she would punish us both.

'I don't want to hear any more!'

We were always yelling at each other, but we loved each other very much. I loved my little brother too. His name was Fahad. At the clinic when he was born, everyone wanted to hold him: my father's mother and my mother's mother, who looked like the prime minister of Bangladesh, and all my aunts, uncles and cousins. Even I was allowed to hold him. I was happy and amazed: I'd never seen such a tiny baby.

I spent more and more of my time playing chess. Every day my father would teach me new things: how to work out moves in advance, how to avoid making mistakes and how to avoid traps. The pieces of this giant jigsaw began to fall into place, the muddle started to sort itself out, and I got better. Soon I was begging my father to enter me for a tournament. I'd heard that the top thirteen players would win lessons from a FIDE World Chess Federation instructor. I was five and had only been playing for two months, but my father quickly agreed.

On the day of the tournament I was excited and

fought like a lion. I won three games out of six. In the last round, my opponent was very laid back. He knew I was a beginner and assumed I wasn't that good. So I took advantage of it and beat him. When I found out I was the thirteenth finalist I was stunned.

My father was so happy he hugged me. His friends had come to watch me play, and they congratulated me and gave me beaming smiles. Back at home, I told my mother the good news. She was really impressed.

My first lesson with the FIDE instructor showed me more about the world of chess: it was a real jungle, with all the jungle's dangers and predators, and all its hiding places and traps. I explored every inch of it, and got on so well that my parents decided to pay for me to have private lessons. Although he'd played every day for 30 years, before long I was beating my father.

I took part in several tournaments in Dhaka, playing against both children and adults. I won trophies and sometimes even medals, and I was so happy to take them home to my mother – except for the time when I left my medal on the bus by mistake, and I was so furious I nearly cried. My parents loved it when I won, but when I lost against weaker players my father would scowl at me. One day he was so angry with me that he refused to take me back for the rest of the championship. My mother asked her brother to drive me instead. Upset, I won the last five rounds. A government minister awarded me the trophy. The newspapers began to talk about me, and I was even on the television.

I was six years old when I asked my father if I could take part in a tournament in India. He agreed, but my mother was horrified:

'But it's too far away! It takes too long to get there! He'll be worn out by the journey! He'll get lost in the streets of Kolkata!'

'*Amma*, it's only for a week. I'll be careful.'

I begged and begged her, and in the end she gave in.

'You won't do anything silly? You'll eat properly? You'll sleep? You won't go out on the streets alone?'

I promised her everything, and ran off to tell the news to the whole neighbourhood. I couldn't wait, I was counting the days. At last the day came when it was time to set off.

Kolkata! I was lost in wonder at this city of riches, with its vast shopping centre, its lights everywhere, its Metro and its smart hotels. Our room had a television and a bathroom.

It was a strange city too. People there spoke Bengali with a peculiar accent that I tried to imitate. There were traffic jams like at home, not because of the traffic but because there were people walking about all over the roads, and cows wandering through the streets wherever they wanted to go. There were lots of other surprising things, like the street sellers offering strange red fruit called strawberries. And I nearly fell over in amazement when I passed a woman on the pavement and she was walking about smoking like a man!

I came second in the championship, and it wasn't difficult to persuade my father to let me go again. A few months later, I was the winner. When I got home, in the middle of the night, my mother ran to me and gave me a big hug.

'*Amma, Amma*, I won the tournament! I beat grown ups! I beat *Indians*!'

Next day, she told the whole neighbourhood about my triumphs. She said that one day I would take part in the world championship, she was sure. People congratulated me. I felt proud.

That evening my father brought the newspapers home. There were stories about me: 'Bangladeshi Boy (7) Wins Kolkata Chess Tournament', and 'A Champion in the Making'!

Life was good.

Chapter 3

MY LIFE IS OVER

XP: *Bangladesh is a young country with a troubled history. East Bengal was first established when Bengal was divided in 1946; when India gained its independence the following year, East Bengal became part of Pakistan. From 1955 it became East Pakistan, and in 1971 it declared independence as Bangladesh. The political life of this new state was punctuated by a succession of military coups, assassination attempts and violent rivalries between the two main parties. It was in the run-up to a presidential election, when political tensions were running particularly high, that more personal events were to impinge directly on Fahim's family and tear his peaceful life apart.*

People were talking on the radio about the coming elections, which were constantly postponed, and about demonstrations. Soon we could hear gunfire in the streets. The army was firing on the protestors. It sounded like there was a war going on. Our parents said we mustn't go out, first of all in the evening because of the curfew, and then, when it got too dangerous, in the daytime too. The streets were deserted.

The grown-ups would talk about what was going on. They were frightened. The more frightened they became, the more they talked. They said the police were hunting down the protestors. That they were going into houses, beating the people who lived there, searching them, turning everything upside down looking for weapons, stealing money. When they found the people they were looking for, they treated them like criminals. They made up robberies, murders, whatever, so that they could arrest them, throw them in prison, and sometimes have them executed.

My father seemed preoccupied. He spent less and less time playing chess and more and more time on the telephone. He talked to people I didn't know. He looked serious. Sometimes I would overhear snatches of his conversations with my uncles or my grandfather, about people who were jealous of the club's success, and about the tournaments I was winning.

Several times people came to our house, forcing their way in and demanding to see my father. They asked lots of questions that I didn't understand. They searched the house, made lots of noise and woke up the baby, who started to cry. Jhorna and I would hide behind our mother. They went away, and then they came back again. They shouted, asking again where my father was, but my mother said nothing and stayed calm, even when the baby really screamed. Before they went away they looked at me, and I was scared. I didn't know what they wanted. After they'd gone my mother went and hid, and I found her crying. That made me angry. No one had the right to hurt my mother. I hated those men. If I'd been bigger, I would have stood up for her. But I didn't even know how to comfort her.

There was a family meeting to discuss it all, with my uncles, aunts and grandparents. One evening, my parents called me into the living room. Looking grave, they explained that I mustn't go outside any more. Not for any reason. Not ever, not even to go to school. Too bad, I could study at home. They explained that some very serious things were happening, and that they were afraid I might be kidnapped. I didn't know what made them think that, but they looked very serious. And things like that did happen in our country. If people wanted to hurt someone, they'd take it out on his son. Ever since I was little I'd heard stories of children being snatched away and never seen again. But this time the child in danger was me. And the only way to avoid the danger was never to set foot outside the house.

In the mornings I would stay inside. In the afternoons, when my friends came home from school, I would be allowed to play in the courtyard. But only in the courtyard. Never in the street. Never anywhere near the street. From the doorway, my mother would watch me constantly.

My life was awful. I was bored. I was frightened. Whenever I looked at my mother, her red-rimmed eyes would make me feel sad. At night I would imagine men pouncing on me, kidnapping me, selling me as a slave in a faraway country where I would never see my family again. When I finally got to sleep, different men, wearing masks and dressed all in black, would come in and stab me to death.

One morning, an anonymous letter arrived. That is, it didn't say who'd sent it, but we knew all the same. My parents didn't read it to me, or even show it to me, but they told me about it. It said that some men were going to kidnap me because I was so good at chess.

I didn't understand why these people were attacking me, I just knew that I was too young to die. That night in bed I heard voices:

'His life is in danger, you must take him far away.'

'But all five of you can't go, you'd be spotted in no time.'

'A family with three children, one a baby, is bound to attract attention.'

'They'll track you down, even in India.'

'You'll need to cover your tracks. If it's just the two of you it will be more discreet.'

'But what will you do for money? Travelling is expensive.'

'Leave the rest of them behind, nothing will happen to them. It's Fahim who's in danger.'

'We'll look after them. Go somewhere safe, you and Fahim. You can send for them later.'

I was outraged. I clenched my fists. I wanted to punch the men who were threatening me, the cowards who were attacking me without daring to show their faces. I didn't want to leave Jhorna and the baby. I didn't want to leave my mother. I couldn't imagine life without her, far from her arms, her voice, her smell, her smile, the way she looked at me.

My father called me into the living room. My mother was pale and silent. My father told me that the next day he and I would have to go away. He said I was too young to understand, but that we had no choice. And I didn't dare to ask any questions.

The neighbours came round. The evening was sad, like when someone has died. Except the dead person was me, and I wasn't dead. Not yet. I'd be dead if I was killed. If I was kidnapped. If I was taken away from my mother.

I cuddled up close to her. I wouldn't leave her. We didn't even think of going to sleep. In the morning, she hugged me tight. She was weeping. Over and over again she kept saying:

'Take care of yourself, my son, I love you. Don't

forget me. May God reunite us very soon. I'll think of you every day. I'll always be with you. You will be in my heart for ever.'

We left. Just the two of us, my father and I. It was 2 September 2008, the worst day of my life.

I was eight years old.

I was lost.

My life was over.

Chapter 4

AN ENDLESS JOURNEY

It was all so confused. In my memory everything is all jumbled up. There were buses. Aeroplanes. Kolkata. New Delhi. Life on the run. Journeys that went on for ever, that put me off travelling for good. My father searching. Making calls. Always making calls. Trying to get as far away from Bangladesh as we could. Embassies, consulates, trying to buy tickets to get out of Asia, far away. So that no one could ever find us. An airport. An ancient Aeroflot plane. A night flight. A stopover in Russia, maybe?

I forgot it all as soon as it happened, blotted it out of my memory. My father and I would never talk about those days and nights, the running away. We'd put it in a box and shut the lid on it. Much later, when I came to work on this book, I would find that my memory had kept all of the pain, but had mixed up everything else. Because that wasn't really what happened.

My father had gone on ahead to make all the arrangements. He wasn't at home to tell me that we had to run away. It must have been one of his brothers. In the morning, it was my uncle, along with my mother, my brother, my sister and my grandmother, who took me to the border, where my father was waiting for us.

So it was on the border with India, far away from Dhaka, that I kissed my mother for the last time. Everyone seemed to be crying: my mother, my grandmother, Jhorna, everyone. Except for me. The only person who didn't cry was me. I don't like to show my feelings. I don't like feelings.

But I don't remember any of it. I've blotted out my memories. Shut them in a box. Even my grief, my overwhelming grief. More impossible to bear with every mile we travelled. Every morning when I woke up. Every night when I went to bed. Every time I had a nightmare. Even the pain. Week after week of pain, month after month, sometimes intense, sometimes dull. I don't remember anything. Anything at all, except the feeling that I would never see my mother again.

To blot out my memories I slept, I slept all the time. Even today I can't talk about the day that I lost my mother. I can't even talk about her.

My father decided we would go and join a friend of his in Madrid. In Spain he was bound to be able to find work and get papers, it would be easy. But he didn't manage to get a visa and we fell back on the Italian embassy: the idea of a father wanting to take his son to Rome seemed normal enough. We got stamps in our passports: free movement for a month in what they called the 'Schengen area'. Apparently the flight was very long for me. Apparently we spent a week in Rome, with a friend of my father. Apparently I was ill. I don't remember anything until our journey took us to Budapest.

It was dawn one morning in October when we got off the bus. All of a sudden the air was so cold I could hardly breathe. It was as though the Hungarians had turned the air-conditioning up full in the streets and the thermostat had got stuck.

Budapest was so different from Dhaka. I examined it eagerly. Everything was clean and tidy. The traffic was orderly and well behaved, even if everyone did insist on driving on the wrong side of the road. It was nothing like the chaos of Dhaka. The people walking along beneath the tall buildings looked strange. Of course I'd seen white people before, in films. Even in real life. But never so many at once.

We wandered around looking for our hotel. In Dhaka, any bus driver could tell you where to go. In Budapest, nobody understood me, even when I asked in my best English, the English I'd learned at school. Nobody had heard of our hotel, and later on nobody had heard of the chess club. When he was in India, my father had entered me for the First Saturday chess tournament in Budapest in October. Although I was so sad, I still felt a little thrill of curiosity at the thought of my first tournament in Europe.

It was raining. We got lucky when a lady went out of her way to show us how to get there. She pointed out a building that was way too quiet. On the other side of the street, outside an official-looking building with a flag flying on it, a soldier was marching up and down, swinging his boots right up to his waist.

The entrance hall was dark. Instinctively I shrank back. My father squeezed my hand. We went up to the first floor. As soon as I opened the door my fear melted away: a crowd of cheerful people turned to look at us. They smiled.

XP: *We can only imagine the world of difference between the Dhaka club that Fahim was used to going to with his father and the offices of the Hungarian Chess Federation. Within this period building in the historic centre of Budapest lay a sequence of small rooms cluttered with tables inlaid with chessboards, jewels of the art of marquetry, and lined with bookcases containing a selection of venerable magazines and a library devoted to the vast literature of chess.*

A bearded giant rushed towards us, his arms flung wide open.

'Hello Mr Nura,' he said in English, lifting my father off his feet. 'I am Nagy Laszlo.'

The organiser of the tournament had never seen my father, because he had communicated with him online. But he couldn't help but recognise us: we were the only non-white people there.

'Do you want a drink? Something to eat?'

He introduced us to the players and the referee, and everyone gave us a warm welcome. They congratulated my father on his courage. Did everyone in Europe know that he'd saved my life?

The tournament lasted a week. There were dozens of players: teenagers, adults, even old people – but no other children. I was the youngest player and also the smallest, and I had to sit on top of a stack of chairs in order to reach the table. I was competing in a group of six players, which meant I played ten games, two against each of my five opponents. With a point for each win and half a point for a draw, I decided to aim for five points, five out of ten.

In the first round, I played against the best player in

my group, a Hungarian who had a bumbag holding secret treasures that I could only guess at. The game didn't last long. He was nice, but you could tell that inside he was angry, especially when I checkmated him. Nagy Laszlo was delighted. He threw his arms around me, and it was my turn to fly up into the air:

'Bravo! Bravo Fahim! You are incredible!'

The Hungarian was surprised. He wasn't happy. In the return match he'd try harder.

My next opponent was an old man. Really old. He had to be at least – I don't know how old. Before we started the game he offered me a sweet. I didn't know him so I said no: I'm not daft. So he unwrapped it and popped it in his mouth. Instantly I wished I'd said yes. He had wrinkles and he shook, which was annoying. I couldn't concentrate. I wasn't great in the next game either.

Then I played a British journalist, who was really nice. She had blonde hair and her name was Diana. She was good. It was a tough game. I captured one of her pieces without giving up anything in return. I had the advantage and I hung on to it. I defended my piece so she couldn't take it. I dodged and feinted and wriggled. The game went on for four hours. Gradually we were reaching stalemate. It was impossible to mount an attack. That extra piece was blocking the way. Finally I gave up

33

and suggested a draw. Fortunately in the next round I got my own back. Putting on my best serious face, I said to Diana:

'You play well. You gave me the hardest time of them all. Can we play again?'

We met up again for friendly games as soon as we could, and we became friends. From then on she would greet me not with a handshake but with a kiss on the cheek, as though we were family.

XP: *Later, in a piece entitled 'Fahim the Conqueror' and published on the Chess News website, Diana Mihajlova wrote:*

'The chess-playing part was easy and tremendously enjoyable, but communication was difficult as the father spoke no word of any European language, though the boy was making the utmost effort with his admirable if broken English. I retain a picture of the two of them – the boy always impeccably groomed and perfectly behaved, the father polite, quiet and visibly over-protective of his child, always hand in hand, as if facing together the menace of this new, frightening world.'

The First Saturday was nearly over. I won the last two rounds against a strange man. In my head I called him Madness. I finished with six-and-a-half points out of ten. The other players congratulated me. I was so happy. I'd beaten my own goal. Now all I wanted to do was go home and tell ... No, I couldn't think about that.

We stayed on in Hungary for a while, and Nagy Laszlo and Diana took turns to show us round Budapest. I liked it. Except for the food, which was bland and tasteless. The only things I liked were the noodles, the burgers and the cakes. I wondered why people in Hungary hardly ever ate rice. At home, a meal without rice was just a snack. Some families even had rice for breakfast.

My father explained to Nagy and Diana that we had to carry on to Madrid. They found us a bus, but it didn't go to Madrid direct: it stopped in France and we would have to change in Paris. I didn't want to go to France, I didn't even want to travel through France. A friend in Bangladesh had told me that in France they eat dogs. I tried to reassure myself by thinking about Zinedine Zidane: perhaps it was eating dog that made him so good? But Zidane or no Zidane, there was no way I was going to eat dog. If I went to France I might starve to death. In which case I might just as well go and die in Bangladesh. I wanted to tell my father, but I didn't dare. So I got on the bus with him, and on 17 October 2008 I got off again at Porte de Bagnolet in Paris. The last stop. France.

Chapter 5

WELCOME TO FRANCE

In France we don't know a soul, but one of my father's friends in Bangladesh has told his cousin that we're coming, and he's there to meet us at the bus station. His name is M. Bamoun. At last, someone who speaks our language! He has lived in the Père-Lachaise district of Paris for twenty years. He is unemployed, and is struggling to make ends meet. But he and his wife put us up on a mattress in their living room all the same: for us, helping each other out is a tradition.

'How old are you, Fahim?'

'Eight.'

'My daughter Alya is the same age as you: you can be friends.'

I can't wait to play with her. But soon I'm stunned by the way she behaves. She uses bad language, and when she wants something she screams at her mother. In Bangladesh no child would dare behave like that. I don't yet know that in France there are lots of parents who let their children behave like little dictators, and no one seems to mind.

We've barely moved in before I fall ill. I'm all yellow and running a fever. I can't swallow anything and I itch all over. I feel so bad I think I'm going to die. It seems so unfair to die so far from home, in a place I don't even know. My father looks after me. He gives me water to drink and watches over me.

A doctor comes. He speaks to M. Bamoun in French. I don't understand a word. He keeps saying Alya's name. But I'm the one who's ill. The doctor examines me and calls me Alya. I'm furious. I'm not a girl! Can't he see that? But I'm too weak to protest. He scribbles obscure words on an orange form, and M. Bamoun looks relieved.

When my temperature drops my father starts getting ready to leave for Spain, but several people advise us to stay. They say that France protects people like us. I like the idea that a country can defend us against our enemies. So my father makes a decision. We'll stay. While we wait for things to calm down in Bangladesh. While we wait to go home. He doesn't ask me what I think, but I agree with him: it doesn't look as though anyone is going to make me eat dog.

Life with the Bamouns is pretty good, especially the meals: Mme Bamoun is a good cook. But the days drag on for ever. I spend all day watching cartoons on television. Luckily you can understand them even if you don't know any French. When Alya comes home from school she switches channels without asking me. To show me who's boss. I'm jealous.

My father and I go out a lot, to meet people and explore the streets. But our visa runs out, and everyone warns us to look out for the police. So we go out less and less, only when we need to. My father's afraid that they might find us and put us on a plane back to Bangladesh. Direct. I imagine the masked men in black who'll be waiting to kill me as I get off the plane. M. Bamoun is scared too, frightened that someone might report him to the authorities. He tells us that in France you can get sent to prison for taking in friends. So he hides us: when visitors come, we wait on the stairs until they've gone.

One day, I'm on the Métro with my father and M. Bamoun. Suddenly three men in navy blue uniforms and caps appear in our carriage. They look like policemen. People are showing them their tickets. M. Bamoun signals to my father, who grabs me by the hand and jumps on to the platform just as the doors are closing. We charge towards the exit. In front of us are two other men, one black and the other white. The train pulls out, accelerates and is swallowed up by the tunnel. We glance over our shoulders and slow down: phew!

Then all of a sudden the two men in front of us

give a start and double back on their tracks: in the passage I can see more men in uniform. Still gripping my hand, my father runs after our two partners in crime. Following their lead, we race down some narrow steps that go down to the Métro tracks. Carried forward by his own momentum, the first man leaps over the rails and is already clambering up on to the platform opposite. My father and I are about to follow him when the other one pulls us back:

'No! It's too dangerous!'

I'm paralysed with fear. What if the policemen come on to the platform? What if they find us here, skulking in the shadows like criminals? And why have the rails suddenly started to judder and make that deafening noise? I flatten myself against the wall. The man checks the platform in the mirror above our heads, and after a moment that feels like an eternity he signals to us that the coast is clear. We climb back up and get on the train that pulls into the station, trying to look natural. At last the bell rings, the doors close and the train starts moving. My legs have turned to jelly and I want to cry, but I don't let it show. I want to squeeze up against my father but I don't dare. Slowly the knots in my stomach start to unwind.

In bed that night I turn things over in my mind. Why didn't my father, who is so honest, buy us tickets for the Métro? Has he run out of money? Over the next few days, I watch him secretly. I listen in when he's on the phone. He says that we can't stay in the Bamouns' living room for ever. When he asks for money – from his friends in Spain and Switzerland and a cousin in Scotland – he sounds embarrassed.

XP: *Undeterred by his total lack of knowledge of the French language and legal system, Nura set out to find a way of staying in France with his son. There was good community support, and he discovered the existence of the right of asylum, a right recognised by the United Nations since 1967, which allows people who are in danger in their own country to seek the hospitality and protection of another country. He learned that France, 'home of the rights of man', had offered asylum for several centuries and viewed it as a national tradition. So it was therefore with complete confidence that he took to the tortuous byways of the French legal system and bureaucracy, embarking on a journey that – given the self-evident nature of his predicament – should have taken just a few months. Other Bangladeshis in Paris pointed him in the direction of the organisation France Terre d'Asile (the name means France, Land of Asylum), set up to provide support for*

asylum seekers, both in making their applications and in their daily lives.

So it was that, after Dhaka, Kolkata, New Delhi, Rome and Budapest, Nura and Fahim found themselves in the Paris suburb of Créteil, a mere stone's throw – as luck would have it – from one of the best chess schools in France.

France Terre d'Asile send us to the Préfecture, a big modern building with windows everywhere: the glass is orange, and to me it looks as though it's holding the sun hostage inside. It must be a magic place, and I hope we'll come back often. As soon as we get inside the illusion is shattered: there are crowds of people waiting, and the minutes crawl by. At last we are seen by a lady with funny red hair who isn't very friendly and gives us a great pile of forms to fill in. Back at home, my father stares in dismay at the long list of questions to which he doesn't know the answers. They ask for names, dates and places that he doesn't know without looking them up. He rummages about in our things, searching for documents and evidence. Then, with M. Bamoun, he writes down our story and describes the problems we had in Bangladesh.

When they've finished, M. Bamoun takes my father

to have it all translated. I don't understand why he can't do it himself, as he speaks good French. He explains that you have to use a translator who has taken an oath.

The next day we go back to Créteil. It's raining, and the house of the sun isn't filled with light any more. In fact it's pretty ugly. When I see all the people waiting inside, I begin to hate the place.

XP: *That day, Nura was given temporary leave to stay, which meant that he and Fahim could legally stay in France for a month, the period needed to verify whether or not his application would be considered. Armed with this, they were given accommodation by France Terre d'Asile, initially in emergency hostels and subsequently, when space became available, at the Centre d'Acceuil pour Demandeurs d'Asile (CADA), the centre for asylum-seekers in Créteil.*

Thus Nura and his son embarked on the obstacle course that awaits all immigrants arriving on French soil. Of course they had absolutely no idea of what lay in store for them. Despite being involved in community work, I too had little notion then of what daily life was like for asylum-seekers, or of the obstacles they had to overcome. It was a subject in which Fahim was to become my teacher.

'The hostel at Créteil is full at the moment.'

The woman picks up the phone and dials 115. After a brief conversation she announces:

'The Samu Social, an organisation that finds accommodation for homeless people, has found you a hotel room.'

M. Bamoun translates. My father stiffens:

'I've run out of money.'

Just as I thought.

'No need to worry. The cost is covered while your application is being processed.'

I think about all the people living on the streets of Dhaka, all the poor people who are homeless. I'd never imagined there might be an organisation that could find them somewhere to stay. Let alone that one day it would be me needing this sort of help.

It's already late when we get to Fresnes. The man on reception shows us the room: it's magnificent, with a television, and in the bathroom a tiny swimming pool called a bath.

Gesturing with his hands, the man asks if we have eaten, and when my father signals 'no', he goes away and comes back with a tin of something. The label says 'sweetened condensed milk', which means nothing to us. But since we're starving we accept it eagerly. My father opens the can. It's full of white, sticky goo. I taste it. Milk, sweet and sickly: yuck! Who could eat that? We throw it away and go to bed hungry.

By the next day I realise that this hotel is not the paradise I thought it was: in fact it's more like a version of hell. During the day we have to get out of the rooms. Even if we have nothing to do, nowhere to go, no official stuff to take care of, no one to go and see. And it's cold. Colder than you can imagine. I have a lovely coat with a red collar that my father had bought me in India, but even with my jumper on underneath it I'm still cold. My father finds a hat and gloves for me. I'm sure it won't be enough to stop me freezing to death.

So we go out as little as possible. We stay in the foyer. All day. With nothing to do. Ten hours a day. Ten long hours of endless boredom. In the foyer. In the corridor. In the icy draughts. Sometimes standing up, sometimes sitting down. Sometimes in front of a television screen showing rolling news bulletins that I don't understand.

We're not the only ones. There are other people waiting with us. People of all ages and colours. People from all over the world who have ended up here by an accident of fate, like us. Occasionally, not very often, they talk. In whispers almost. As if it's against the rules. They speak in languages I don't understand. We can't even communicate with each other: we come from different corners of the globe.

I'm raging. I want to go back to our room, to sleep, have a shower, warm up. To play chess with my father. But I don't complain: I can see that he's fed up too. I don't want to heap my unhappiness on top of his. So I keep quiet. And I wait.

We only go out when we need to buy something to eat: a little rice, chicken or fish. Then we have to wait ages for our turn to use the kitchen. When the food is ready, we eat. My father cooks well. Though obviously not as well as ...

When evening comes at last, we go up to our room. I go straight to bed and fall asleep. To forget.

After a month, we go to a different hotel. Out towards Valenton. It's a day I'll never forget. I'd never seen snow before. I'd heard a lot about it and I couldn't wait to see it. People in France are lucky. Well, that day it was snowing. Really snowing. And it didn't take me long to realise that I detested it: it was freezing cold, the pavements were all slippery, and we struggled with our cases. Now I could see that snow was completely pointless, that it was just a pain for everyone.

We had to find the bus station, the bus for Valenton, the stop to get off at, the hotel. It's so hard living in a country when you don't speak the language!

At Valenton, our life gets better. We're allowed to stay in our rooms. So I flop in front of the television. I drug myself up with cartoons and mangas. When I've had enough, I turn the TV off and do nothing. I stretch out and think. I'd like to have friends. To play with them. Is it possible to have friends in France?

The hotel is in a remote district miles from anywhere, where there's nothing to do and the streets are deserted. There's a massive shopping centre, but it's always empty. I wonder how the people who work there earn a living. My father and I go there regularly to buy provisions. Since we don't have a refrigerator, we keep our food on the windowsill. In Bangladesh it would go off in no time.

We get to know a Bangladeshi couple at the hotel. They arrived on the same day as us, and will leave with us too. I don't know yet that they will get their papers long before we do. I like them: we speak the same language. They and my father talk together. I hear them say that we may be in France for a long time. A very long time.

That I might have to live here for ever. That I might never go home again.

So I decide to live a life with no regrets, not to look back to the past any more, not to think about Bangladesh any more.

A month later the news comes. They're expecting us at the Créteil hostel. Another move, more chaos. It's pouring with rain. The gutters in the street are overflowing. Our bags are heavy. We're soaked.

As we arrive at the hostel, a handful of people in the foyer watch us vaguely. A woman smiles at us. I feel intimidated. My father makes straight for the reception desk. A man arrives: he's tall and he's called Muhamad. He shakes our hands warmly and quickly jots down some notes before giving us some things: two toothbrushes, toothpaste, soap, a broom, toilet paper and 45 euros. We're rich again!

We follow Muhamad up some stairs and along a corridor that's horrible and running with water, with pails and floor cloths in the middle, dustbins in a corner, and all sorts of stuff piled up at the far end. He opens a door with numbers on it that I recognise from my English lessons at school: 123, easy to remember. This is our room. It's small, with bunk beds. I choose the bottom one. There's also a table and two chairs, a wardrobe, a washbasin and a refrigerator. Outside the window, between two tall buildings, the bare branches of a tree are swaying. My father seems pleased. The room is clean, the walls are white and spotless. He likes it when things are clean and tidy. He detests cockroaches. So do I.

While my father unpacks our bags, I go off to explore. The corridor has dried out and doesn't look such a mess. The building is quiet. Too quiet. Like everywhere else in France, there are no children to be seen. I open doors and look inside. I find the bathroom and toilets, which are a bit dirty and disgusting. But Muhamad is back already, and takes us downstairs to a big room full of tables and chairs.

'This is the canteen, CANTEEN. This is where you'll come to eat for the moment.'

The hours pass, quietly, slowly, pointlessly. And then – then I hear a vague murmur, footsteps, noises getting louder, people chasing each other, a stampede, shouts, voices – children! It's five o'clock. Success! Friends!

I race out to meet them. By a stroke of luck there's a Bangladeshi boy, Hadi. He introduces me to the rest of them, and straight away I'm one of the gang. Some of them speak good French. I admire that. Maybe one day I will too. We play games – not cricket or badminton but football and tag. On fine days we play outside, behind the building. On rainy days we hang about on the stairs. Sometimes we play outside even so and get soaked and are told off by our parents. But we do it again anyway.

In the morning my friends go off to school, and I wait. I'm impatient. When the clock says the school day is over, life will begin again for me. The older boys arrive back first, then the younger ones who are at primary school. Maybe in France the older you are, the less you have to work?

Muhamad puts my name down to go to school. On my first day, my friends show us the way. I'm happy not to be left all alone in the hostel any more. The head teacher meets us at the school door. His name is Jean-Michel. He has white hair that makes him look old, and jeans that make him look young. I've never seen a head teacher wearing jeans before.

Jean-Michel takes me into the playground. There are children running in all directions, but I'm not fazed. I'm not easily fazed. Plus I recognise some of them from the hostel. When break is over, Jean-Michel takes me into Mme Faustine's class, which is for children who don't speak French. Then he takes me into Mme Klein's class for eight- and nine-year-olds. Then we go back to Mme Faustine's class. I'm not sure whose class I'm in.

Mme Faustine tells me to sit down. There are only ten children in the class: two Chinese girls, a Sri Lankan boy who lives at the hostel, a Chechen boy who is also from the hostel, two black boys, a fair-haired boy, a weird boy from I never find out where, a chubby girl and a wimp. Mme Faustine gives me some colouring to do. I take my time, as I'm in no rush to start work. When I've finished, she tells me the picture is of Father Christmas. She makes me say it after her. FATHER CHRISTMAS. I've never heard of Christmas. In Bangladesh we celebrate Eid.

I have lunch in the canteen. The dinner lady serves me a sort of white sausage, peculiar and not particularly nice-looking. One of my friends explains something to me but I don't really understand: I think it's a special sausage for Muslims.

After lunch, Mme Faustine puts a sheet of paper on my table. There are blanks to fill in. I glance at it, then look up at the teacher in surprise. It's so easy that for a moment I think she must be making fun of me. But no, she keeps a straight face. So I take my time. I'm not frightened of her: Alya's mother told me that teachers in France never hit their pupils, even when they get things wrong.

The next morning I'm not so eager to go to school. My father wakes me up quietly. Then loudly. Then he shakes me. Then he gets cross. I can't stay in bed any longer. I start the day in a bad mood. The journey's over. Life goes on.

Chapter 6

A TRUE DISCOVERY

Even when we were still at the Bamouns my father would look all serious and say:

'Fahim, I didn't bring you halfway round the world so that you could watch cartoons.'

In November, he bought a French book on chess for me. I couldn't understand the French text, obviously, but I would look at the diagrams and try to work out the problems. More importantly, he decided to find a club where I could play. This wasn't easy, as neither of us spoke French, and the Bamouns knew nothing about chess. But eventually he found a club called 'La Tour Blanche'.

To begin with I didn't like it: it was nearly all adults there, and I couldn't understand what they were saying. But I carried on going there, even after we moved out to the suburbs.

In December I played in a tournament. I liked being back in the competitive atmosphere, and I was eager for the fight and for the pleasure of playing against new opponents. With eight wins and a draw, I was the winner. I felt proud. My father was over the moon. Both for my success and for the cheque for the 70 euro prize money.

At the awards ceremony, a man came over to speak to us. When he realised that we didn't understand what he was saying, he repeated himself slowly. My father made out 'club' and I grasped 'Créteil'. The man scribbled a quick note and wrote down an address.

Once we've settled in at the hostel, we decide to go and find this club in Créteil. We ask the people at the hostel, and Hadi translates. The club is in a street with a name. This always amazes me, as streets at home don't have names.

'It's easy,' they say. 'It's near those funny buildings that look like cabbages called Les Choux de Créteil.'

My father and I set off to find it. We look everywhere, go round in circles, get it wrong, get lost, and before we know it it's dark. It's really hard to find your way in Europe. When at last we arrive outside the building it's late. It's in darkness, the door is shut and the metal shutter is pulled down.

'Is this where it is, do you think?' asks my father.

I'm disappointed:

'It doesn't look like a chess club.'

I look at the sign beside the door.

'Wait!'

I point.

'I know that word. It's on the cover of the book you gave me. I think it says "chess".'

We feel more hopeful again, and the next day we go back. Earlier. The club is open. A man stands in the doorway; he's tall and thin and smoking. He smiles at us. My father gives him the note. The man reads it and looks interested, then tries to explain:

'There's no one here today. You'll have to come back.'

He waves his hands about, then goes off to find a calendar:

'Saturday. Come back on Saturday. There's a lesson at eleven o'clock.'

We go away. I'm really disappointed. It's pathetic, this club. Either it's shut or there's no one there. There's nothing going on, it's dead. And it looks cramped and shabby. We've got to find another club, but I don't dare tell my father.

Third time lucky. We go back on Saturday. The man teaching the lesson looks just like Nagy Laszlo. I'm surprised. He doesn't look like a trainer. A trainer should be young, slim, clean-shaven. He's the complete opposite. He has a big paunch and a beard, and he looks at least 70!

He looks up:

'Hello?'

Another surprise. I'm expecting the voice of a little old man, weak and shaky, to match his grey hair. But his voice is loud and booming. I know at once that I will never get on with this man.

'You must be Fahim?'

Hearing my name I nod, feeling a bit shy.

'I'm Xavier.'

He beckons me to come closer. The club members are looking in silent concentration at the projected image of a large chessboard. Xavier takes me through the problem on his computer. I think about it. I know the answer, but I don't know how to say it. So I point with my index finger as though I'm moving the pieces, one by one. Xavier smiles and turns to his pupils. He asks questions and they answer them. Words, words and more words piling up, mountains of words that I can't understand. The lesson goes on for ages. I'm bored. Then the pieces on the wall begin to move, and I watch intently. Then they start talking again, and I'm bored once more.

I turn to my father:

'Can we go now?'

'Don't you want to watch the exercises?'

I try to persuade him:

'No, it's too easy, I want to go.'

'OK, let's go.'

But Xavier signals to us to wait, and my father sits down again. Too bad! When the lesson is finally over, I try to slip outside. Xavier keeps my father back and suggests we meet up the following Tuesday. I hope my father will refuse, but he agrees.

It's too late for lunch in the canteen. On the way back, my father buys me a sort of sandwich with hot meat in it, called a kebab. I know that today I've made a true discovery. Kebabs and I were made for each other!

XP: *When he first arrived at the club, Fahim was only eight. I remember a serious child – too serious perhaps – with eyes shining with curiosity. Whenever I spoke he frowned, as if to work out what I was saying, then looked question-ingly at his father. This little boy from halfway across the world seemed lost.*

A few days earlier, my colleague Patrick had mentioned that an 'exceptionally gifted' child (that was what the note said) had arrived from the Indian subcontinent. It irritated me, as every week people tell me about some new prodigy. So it was with considerable reservations that I greeted him when he arrived – late – at my lesson. My students, all of them older, were preparing for a high-level champion-ship, and were stumped by a problem designed to test their spatial awareness. Fahim was at least four years younger than them, but he surprised me. Instantly, he found the geometrical key to the problem. I knew then that this boy had the makings of a champion.

On Tuesday I go back to the club, dragging my feet. I don't want to see Xavier again, let alone work with him. But I don't have the heart to disappoint my father. He seems so pleased to have found me a trainer. Xavier (or *Ex*avier, as my father will always call him) is waiting for us. He gestures to me to sit down and we start to play. It's hard but exciting. I make mistakes and lose quite a few games, which makes me cross and all the more determined to fight back.

Time passes. What a funny teacher! We just play, and he doesn't say anything: no remarks, no advice. He just thinks about the game, twiddling his beard between his fingers. I'm a bit thrown, but pleased: I don't like it when people tell me how to play.

It's evening. We've been here for hours and I haven't noticed the time slipping past. Xavier wants to fix a time to meet up again, but my father is embarrassed. With a few gestures, Xavier makes him understand that there is nothing for him to pay. I see him differently now: in the end, I can see that we'll get on well together.

From now on, I go to the club several times a week. Xavier gives me problems to solve by arranging pieces on a chessboard. While I solve one problem, he sets up another one. Then we play.

XP: *When I think back to those early games it makes me feel quite emotional. Fahim had been coached intensively by his father and his early teachers, and showed real potential. He had an astonishing ability to concentrate, extraordinary gifts for mental arithmetic and the geometrical perception of space, and a remarkable memory, all of which enabled him to put multiple moves together in advance and to plan well ahead. For such a little chap, he had an unbelievable mental overview of the game.*

I often quote Plato: 'You can discover more about a person in an hour of play than in an hour of conversation.' It was perfectly clear already that this child, who spoke a different language from me and with whom my only means of communication was through playing and watching, was a shrewd tactician, alert to the slightest errors on his opponent's part and capable of deploying a range of strategies that is rare in one so young.

Fate, if such a thing exists, had put this child in my path for a reason. Forced by his chess-playing abilities to leave his home on the other side of the world, he had chanced to end up just a kilometre away from the club. I had to take him under my wing: 'If you refuse to teach a man who possesses the right disposition, you lose a man. If you teach a man who does not possess the right disposition, you lose your teaching. A wise man loses neither men nor his teachings.' I am a great admirer of Confucius.

To begin with it wasn't easy, all the same. The chessboard was our sole means of communication. For tactics this wasn't a problem. But for working on the subtleties of the game it was impossible. How can you explain the complexities of these things through hand gestures? Fortunately, Fahim picked up French at a rate that was quite astounding.

Xavier teaches me the French names of the pieces – the queen was a mere lady (*dame*) and the bishops fools (*fous*) – and technical vocabulary such as the term for a 'pin' (*clouage*) and 'promotion' when a pawn reaches the other side of the board. He shows me when you have to sacrifice a piece to put yourself in a position of strength, why I shouldn't play my queen too early in the game, tricks for stopping my opponent from castling, and how to avoid traps for beginners.

Gradually the club wakes up. The place livens up and the atmosphere is more welcoming, with nice people and lots of children, running around, shouting, laughing, playing. I like it.

As well as doing one-on-one training, I also take part

in coaching for the competition. I get to know the others in my group: Keigo, small and half-Japanese; a girl called Cécile; tall Louis, called Loulou by everyone; another Louis, Chinese with glasses; and his sister Charlotte, who looks exactly like him and wears the same glasses. I make friends with all of them, especially Chinese Louis. We're always together, sitting next to each other during coaching, waiting for each other before it starts and playing chess together afterwards. We communicate as best we can. When we play, he often tries to soften me up by proposing a draw in Bengali:

'*Shoman shoman*?'

Certainly not! We fight to the end! In Chinese (sort of, anyway) I shoot back:

'*No ping du*!'

One day I arrive late for a tournament and everyone has already had lunch. There's nothing left. Chinese Louis gives me his KitKat and is instantly one of my best friends in France. But our friendship isn't to last. Soon after this he stops playing chess and disappears from my life.

My lessons are getting more and more amazing. Xavier is nothing like any chess coach I've ever known. Behind his grizzled beard, he's anything but a boring old teacher. He smokes cigars and rides a motorbike. He's laid back, cool and funny, full of life and fun.

At first I don't understand his jokes, but I like watching the others laughing at them. Then I begin to grasp a few words, a few phrases, and finally everything. Well, nearly everything.

'Frankly, Charlotte, your variant is camel's piss.'

'Variant' I knew, but 'camel's piss'?

'Cécile, if you pull back your king it will be as disastrous as the Flight to Varennes during the Revolution.'

Or:

'Bravo Louis and Loulou, my two *louis d'or*!'

What about me, could I be his '*Fahim d'or*'?

Xavier loves his quotations, particularly Chinese sayings.

'Well done Keigo! Now you're getting interesting, kid! You've worked out that "the greatest generals are those who gain victory without giving battle".'

'Was it Confucius who said that?'

'No, it was Mencius.'

'Whatever, it's always either Mencius or Confucius with you.'

'Or Lao Tzu.'

Everyone bursts out laughing.

Xavier doesn't just teach us chess, he tells us all the

stories that go with it too. He's the type of coach who can spot a position played years ago in a historic game – he must know them all – in a nano-second, and who can then effortlessly slip in some anecdote to do with it.

'Tell Fahim the story of Bobby Fischer and the journalist!'

'Why don't you tell him?'

'You'll like this one, Fahim. A journalist was interviewing Bobby Fischer – you know, the world champion – and asked him, "What do you talk about with your opponent?" To which Fischer replied: "When I arrive I say hello. When I leave I say checkmate."'

Sometimes, especially when everyone wants to answer a question at once, Xavier raises his voice:

'Woah! Shouting won't make your moves any better. Chess is like life: shouting louder doesn't put you in the right. That's why it's so interesting.'

But hidden behind that scary booming voice is a really good guy.

XP: *A few days after I first met Fahim and Nura, I remember I went to see the film* Welcome, *the story of a young asylum-seeker in Calais who decides to learn to swim in order to get across the Channel to England, and of his*

swimming teacher, who is prosecuted for the 'crime' of helping an asylum-seeker. Like many others, I'd been appalled to discover that there was a law that made it illegal to offer someone hospitality, a law that turned normal human values on their head.

It was a period when there was a lot of talk about 'selective' immigration and national identity, and there were mass expulsions of Roma people. France seemed to be able to remember the first part of the Socialist politician Michel Rocard's famous pronouncement on immigration ('France cannot take in all the world's poor and dispossessed …') while conveniently forgetting the second part ('… but she should be proud to play her part').

When I came out of the cinema, I had the impression that the film was carrying on in real life, for me and my young pupil. From the outset, my involvement had gone beyond simply teaching him to play chess.

During the spring holidays, I took Fahim and his father on a long walk through Paris. We went up to the top of the Eiffel Tower, then we walked through the Trocadéro gardens, Place de l'Etoile and the Tuileries. I remember Fahim's expression of amazement as he stood looking up at the Eiffel Tower, and his puzzlement at the trees pruned into square shapes on the Champs Elysées.

Along the way, I tried to tell them about some of the major events in French history: the Napoleonic victories symbolised by the Arc de Triomphe, the guillotine that stood on what is now Place de la Concorde, the Palais Royal that used to stand in the Tuileries. I began to realise what a vast cultural gulf lay between us: neither Fahim nor his father had ever heard of the French Revolution or the rights of man, nor of major figures from outside France such as Hitler and Stalin.

At the end of the afternoon we stopped for a while beside the Seine, worn out. Ignoring all our difficulties in communicating with each other, I just went for it, and promised them that I would never let them down, that they could always count on me. When things have got tough, I've often thought back to my 'Eiffel Tower oath'.

Chapter 7

SPRING, SUMMER, SETBACK

My second day at school and it's all gone wrong already. The morning drags on for ever. At lunchtime all the others go off to the canteen. I'm on my own in the covered part of the playground when the 'weirdo' in my class turns up. He shoves me up against the wall and tries to choke me. He's raging and screaming at me. I have no idea what he's on about. I pretend I don't care and just shrug my shoulders.

Then after a bit I've had enough. Now it's my turn to lose it, and I throw a punch at him. A direct hit! He's down! To make sure he doesn't get back up I sit on top of him, but then he starts to yell and I'm worried about getting into trouble. So I get off him and head for the canteen. Then he jumps me from behind and knocks me over, the coward. He's stronger than me. In the end I give up. He says sorry and we go to the canteen together. After that he respects me; he even becomes my friend.

It's my first fight. My first proper fight. In Bangladesh I'd had a few scraps with my friends, but only in fun. I had an enemy, but we'd never had a fight. Luckily no one's seen us, so I don't get punished.

My third day, and school closes for the 'February holiday'. Yay! I'll be able to spend most of it playing chess and football. Unluckily, during a game of football one of the big boys at the hostel kicks my foot instead of the ball: I feel a terrific pain and instantly the trainer on

70

that foot starts to shrink. My father takes me to hospital, where we have to wait for ages – in France you always have to wait. I have an X-ray, and the doctor tells me I've broken my foot. I get an awesome plaster, which is hot when it goes on and really tight. I have to drag it around for the whole of the holiday, which means I can't run. And it makes my foot shrink: when it comes off my trainer is far too big.

Back to school. The teacher, Mme Faustine, shows me things and teaches me their names: cheek, ear, mouth and eyes, cat, dog and bird. Then it's my turn to say things: trousers, jumper and sock, table, chair and exercise book.

Mme Faustine is strict, and she's always getting cross. One day, when she finds out that Lujai the Sri Lankan boy hasn't done his homework, she's so angry that she knocks his table over. None of us makes a sound. No one dares to move. I never get into trouble. I'm good: I don't muck about or talk in class. I don't speak French, in any case. None of us talk in class because none of us can speak French.

We are all given different work to do. Since I've already been to school, Mme Faustine gives me exercises

71

to do on my own. Some of the others have never been to school before coming to France. For them it's hard. It takes them ages to pick things up. Some of them smile a lot, some of them are sad. Some try to speak, but most of them don't say a word. Some of them are even frightened: you can see it in their faces.

I learn French quickly. It's easy.

I learn to say my name and write it, to count, to understand what people are saying and to read stories.

I learn colours, the days of the week, the alphabet, masculine and feminine and verbs.

I learn what different instructions mean: colour in, cut out, put a cross, copy, read, write, cross out, repeat, glue and draw round.

I learn the difference between a river and a stream, a stone and a pebble, a house and a family, day and night, sadness and fear.

I learn sheep, lamb and ... ewe; bull, calf and ... cow; father, child and ... mother.

I learn the difference between *tu* and *vous*. When I go to the club, I decide to say *vous* to Xavier. It's more respectful, classier.

By March I can understand everything.

By April I can make people understand me.

By May I've lost my accent, but I'm still quiet and shy.

By June I'm fluent, even if I still make little mistakes.

French is helpful. I can talk to my friends. All of them except Sohan, my best friend, who doesn't understand French. I try to help him, but at the end of the year he goes to live in the south of France, and he disappears from my life too.

Maths is simple. Except for problems to begin with, when I don't understand the instructions in French. English is easy. French children are only taught a few words, but I can speak it already.

We do art too. And music. I wonder what the point of it is. We learn songs to put on a show, a 'musical comedy'. My father is surprised and not very happy: he'd rather I was either working hard at school or playing chess.

We do PE too. We have to fence. It's dumb. You have to hold a metal stick and follow all sorts of complicated rules. You aren't allowed to hit anyone properly, in case they get hurt. I try to anyway. Mme Klein gets cross with me and sends me out of the class.

Every day after school my father comes to meet me with

a cake and a carton of fruit juice. We walk back to the hostel with the other children who live there and their parents. We play football, then Yolande comes to make sure we do our homework.

I like living in the hostel. There's room to move, play and run about. Even if it's noisy, even if you have to share the toilets and showers, and even if it isn't a proper home. At least we have a roof over our heads. It seems that there are some people who don't, even though France is a rich country. I'm happy to live at the hostel until I get my own home. I wouldn't like to sleep on the streets. Thank goodness I'll never have to!

XP: *With Fahim, I discovered what daily life was really like for political refugees. The France Terre d'Asile hostel in Créteil is the oldest hostel for asylum-seekers in France, and also one of the largest and best. It is run by 30 or so permanent staff, including Muhamad – Fahim and Nura's social worker – and Frédéric, known as Fred, who is in charge of applications and other paperwork.*

The hostel offers accommodation to over 200 people, and during the day helps many more to negotiate the labyrinthine complexities of official bureaucracy, or simply with the necessities of daily life. It has a kitchen, showers and washing machines that they can use. It's a strange sort of world in microcosm, a sort of Noah's Ark of humanity, where you may come across men, women and children of all types and nationalities, young and old, families and single people: a real Tower of Babel, echoing with every language you can think of. At this point there were more Bangladeshi asylum-seekers in France than any other nationality, and there were several Bangladeshi families living at the hostel.

More than neighbours yet not quite a community, living more intimately than side by side but not quite cohering as a group, these people live their separate lives, see to their affairs, do their housework, cook for themselves and submit the forms and paperwork they are asked for. But they also make friends, set up support networks and display an instinctive solidarity with each other – translating for newcomers and passing on useful tips – before they are forced apart again, as the currents of life sweep them on to different shores.

You have to get to the canteen on time, pick up a tray and join the queue. In the morning my father goes down without me, as I'm not hungry. When I don't have school, I have lunch with him. In the evening, we take our tray up to our room as we like to eat late. The man who dishes out the food isn't fair. He gives bigger portions to pretty women and to people from certain countries. He tips them off when there's something good coming up, and when we get there there's none left. People in the queue moan about it, but my father never says anything, so I don't either.

Gradually I get used to French food. I like the grilled chicken legs, gateaux, strawberries, kiwi fruit, cherries and apricots. I don't like tomatoes or onions – I leave them on the side of my plate – carrots and petits pois when they're all mixed up together, or artichokes. I don't like the bread either: it's cold, like it's mouldy. I refuse to eat merguez (which are all long and thin and disgusting) or figs (which are ugly looking). And most of all I hate being forced to eat anything, like I am at school.

After two months at the hostel we aren't allowed to eat at the canteen any more, and like the others we're given money to cook for ourselves. My father's good at looking after us. He cleans and tidies the room, does the shopping, cooks our meals, does the washing up and washes and irons our clothes. In Bangladesh he used to pay a woman to do all that. Now he does it himself, and he does it brilliantly. I am always well dressed with my hair neatly combed. I often hear the people who run the hostel say things like:

'He looks after his son so well!'

'Have you seen how clean and tidy their room is? You could eat off the floor.'

'At least that poor child has the good luck to have a father like that.'

'What a perfect family, look how attentive his father is!'

My father is quiet and discreet. He's popular with our neighbours. They are from Sri Lanka, Armenia, Pakistan, Ethiopia and Iraq. Not all of them are as quiet as us. There are two women on our floor, one from an African country and the other from Chechnya, who have rows every day. They fight over their children, over crumbs left in the kitchen or over dirty toilets, and they scream and yell and pull each other's hair. Sometimes my father tries to pull them apart, and then they hit him instead.

One day they're fighting with a broom when it hits me on the hand. One of my fingers swells up and turns blue. I'm so angry and think my finger might be permanently bent. Another time the old witches gang up on me: they shout at me and tell my father I've made the corridor dirty. It isn't true, but my father believes them and gives me a slap. After that I hate them.

There's an Armenian couple who have fights in the evening. You can hear them hitting each other in their room. He hits her, and she hits him. Every night. It's violent. The neighbours are worried and cluster outside in the corridor, but no one dares to interfere. I wonder why they stay together if they hate each other so much. When the noise stops, we hear whispering. In the morning, the woman goes out to do whatever she has to do as if nothing has happened.

In another family it's the daughter who gets hit. She's the same age as me, and her mother makes her do everything: the cooking, the housework and the washing. She's never allowed out. When her older brother tries to defend her, the mother locks the door so she can beat her daughter in peace. One evening he was desperate to help her and banged on the door so hard that he broke it.

Fortunately most people are nice. I like Muhamad, who works at the hostel. He's there when we need help. Sometimes he asks me to help him out, and I go to his office to translate when a new Bangladeshi family arrives. He always gives me a Coke.

Like me, my father goes to school: he has French lessons. He never misses a lesson, and is absolutely determined to learn the language in order to 'integrate'. But he makes lots of mistakes and gets his words muddled up. For instance, one lunchtime in the canteen he hears someone say:

'*Bon appétit!*'

So after that he says it all the time to everyone, in the lobby, on the stairs, in the garden:

'*Bon appétit! Bon appétit! Bon appétit!*'

He thinks it means 'hello'. It makes me laugh.

XP: *At first I thought Nura wasn't making much effort to learn French. While his son was bilingual within a matter of months, Nura had difficulty following what was being said and found it difficult to string even two or three words together to make himself understood. Even now his French is still rudimentary. He understands what people say to him, though you're never quite sure to what degree. He can make himself understood in daily life, but he finds it difficult to discuss more complex matters.*

Yet in fact Nura was assiduous in attending the numerous French lessons that were laid on at the hostel and at other community centres in Créteil. He would spend long hours hunched over the books that I passed on to him, and I even funded some private lessons for him – with a Bulgarian as his teacher. The truth was that the one thing that would have helped Nura's language skills to take off was spending time in a French-speaking environment, surrounded by colleagues, friends and neighbours who spoke French. And at that time he had access to none of this. As time went on, I began to realise just how stupendous an effort of will it had cost him to achieve as much as he had. It was a predicament in which he was by no means alone. People from Mali and Senegal, who are used to hearing several languages that share a structure not dissimilar to French, find French much easier to learn. People from Bangladesh and Sri Lanka, by contrast, speak languages that bear so little resemblance to French in their structure – not to speak of their written forms and ways of thought – that they often struggle. Moreover, Nura was 45 and had never learned any language apart from his native Bengali, with the exception of a little basic English. So for him the idea of learning another language was a completely foreign concept.

How many times did I look at Nura and wonder how lonely he must feel, so far away from his family, his friends and his place in Bangladeshi society; looked at askance by so many people; locked into his own language, culture and hopes; and with his only chance of a future – and his only companionship – resting on an eight-year-old child.

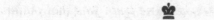

After school, in the hostel corridors, in the kitchen, the only thing the adults ever talk about is their 'papers'. It's one word everyone knows, even people who can barely understand any French. My father is doing everything he possibly can to get papers for us. It's taking him ages for all sorts of reasons: he has to get hold of documents from Bangladesh; the offices out there close down every time there's a demonstration; the post is slow; my father doesn't want to give them our address in France; and everything has to be translated.

When finally he's managed to get everything together, we go to the OFPRA, the French government department dealing with refugees and stateless people. When we get there, we have to take a ticket and wait in a big room with loads of other people. As the ticket numbers come up they appear on a small screen. It takes ages for them to change, even when I stop looking. Also I'm worried: what if I don't understand the questions they ask us?

By the time our number eventually comes up it's lunchtime. Too late! We'll have to come back. The next day we have to wait all over again, until a lady hands us a 'receipt' that allows us to stay in France while our application is being considered. Three months later, a letter

arrives by recorded delivery giving us another appointment. This time we see a lady who gives us another
appointment a month later. I'm at school that day, so
my father goes by himself.

He comes back late that afternoon looking puzzled.
He's seen the lady, this time with an interpreter. To start
off with she asked him simple questions: his name, my
name, his date of birth, my date of birth, etc. After that
my father got confused, because the interpreter was
Indian and didn't speak much Bengali. He stumbled
when he tried to translate what my father said to the
lady, and when he translated what the lady said, my
father couldn't understand what he was saying. After
the first question, my father said:

'I don't understand.'

The interpreter translated, and the lady looked surprised. The question seemed to hover in the air, hanging
over my father's head. It seemed as if it was really important. Then the lady said:

'What's your job?'

'I used to be a fireman. Then I set up a small car
business.'

Years later I read the translation of this, as given by
the interpreter:

'I used to be a fireman. *Then I set up a car dealership
in Germany.*'

'A car dealership?' asked the lady.

'I rented cars out by the day.'

'Did you import the cars from Germany?'

My father was surprised at this. He explained:

'No, it was a business in Bangladesh.'

'So what was the connection with Germany?'

'There wasn't one.'

My father frowned: why was she asking about Germany?

The lady looked at him in astonishment: what was he concealing from her about his car imports from Germany?

After that, she focused her questions on our problems in Bangladesh.

As my father was giving his answers, the interpreter would suddenly cut across him:

'Don't say that. No, that's no good for your application. Wait, I'll say it another way. You mustn't say that sort of thing. It's better if I say something else.'

He argued with my father, interrupted him, butted in when he was in the middle of answering, made him lose his thread, cut across his conversation with the lady, changed his replies. My father was getting annoyed. The lady, who couldn't understand anything of what was going on, was starting to get suspicious.

At the end of the interview, my father returned to the original problem:

'I didn't understand the first question, at the beginning.'

But it was too late, the lady had made up her mind:

'I asked you why you had left your own country. You said, "I don't know."'

Later on at the hostel, when my father talked about what happened, the Bangladeshis there told him some surprising things:

'You know, Nura, there are some Indians who try to pass themselves off as Bangladeshis in order to seek asylum in France. Before you arrived, there was an Indian in the hostel who managed to get his visa that way. Maybe the interpreter was trying to sabotage your application so as to give more chance to people from his own country?'

Summer is here. At school, some of the children start to talk about their holidays. The children from the hostel say nothing. After coaching one evening, Xavier asks:

'Fahim, would you like to come and spend the month of July with me in Brittany?'

'Brittany? What's that?'

'It's a region in western France. My mother has a house there. I take a few pupils there every year. We relax, have fun and compete in the Plancoët tournament.'

This makes me happy. My father too: he's invited as well and he really likes 'Exavier'.

'Who'll be there?'

'Quentin. And Olivier and his mother and sister – they've rented a gîte nearby.'

Our holiday in Brittany is fantastic. Marie-Jeanne, Xavier's mother, is like him: she looks ancient, but in fact she's really nice, good fun and full of life. She has only one fault, but it's a big one: she smokes all the time, and it makes the house smell awful. It's a big, untidy house: the opposite of our own room at the hostel. My father and I sleep with the others in the dormitory on the first floor, while Xavier sleeps in a caravan in the garden.

Every morning he takes me to the beach. The first day I can hardly wait. I long to go swimming, and the sea is so vast and beautiful! I tear down the beach, but when my feet hit the water I get a big shock: it's absolutely freezing! As consolation I tell myself it's dangerous, because I can't swim yet.

In the afternoons we play chess. At the Plancoët tournament I score four points out of nine and win a fine cup. I'll keep it in my room at the hostel.

In the evening we get excited and play all sorts of

games before supper; we play tricks on each other and collapse in fits of giggles. I learn how to play a game with Tarot cards, in which each player is dealt a big hand and you have to try to take the 'kitty'. When it gets dark, Xavier – who's a great film fan – hangs a sheet up in the garage and invites round the neighbours, an elderly couple who live next door and an English couple who never stop talking. He's brought the video projector that he uses for our lessons, and he calls it his 'Cinema Paradiso'.

On 26 July it's my birthday. I'm nine years old.

'Xavier, how old are you?'

I'm amazed to discover that he's only as old as my father: with his beard and white hair I thought he was much older. Xavier gives me a bicycle and teaches me to ride it. I love it! Hills are tough, though.

'Xavier, I know why the Tour de France doesn't go through Brittany.'

'Why not?'

'Because the hills are too steep.'

When we get back to Créteil there's a letter waiting for us: our asylum application has been refused. My father isn't surprised: Frédéric has told him this always happens first time round. So he isn't worried. Nor am I. He and Frédéric prepare a new application to present to the tribunal: thicker and fuller, with more documents and details. Together they fill out stacks of forms, write dozens of letters, make mountains of photocopies. Everything has to be translated, which costs a lot. But everyone is confident. Next time we'll be granted asylum.

Chapter 8

MY SECRET DREAM

In September I'm moved up into the mainstream class at school, along with Stéphanie. Most children stay in the special class for non-French speakers for at least a year. But Mme Faustine and the head teacher have explained to me that I'm ready to join the others and do the same lessons as them.

From day one I'm bored. Everything's too easy. It's just like in Bangladesh: the teachers make a big fuss about saying things that are completely obvious. Useless. Annoying. They ask us pointless questions, and make us read books that bore us all to tears and then ask us stupid questions about them. I hate school. I don't even like going swimming: you can't just splash around, you have to learn to swim, and they're always making us get out of the water and stand around waiting, and I get cold.

There's only one thing I look forward to, and that's going to the chess club. On coaching evenings things always follow the same routine. When we arrive, Xavier talks to my father – or at least he tries to. He asks him about our life and how things are going. My father tells him proudly about my school marks and shows him my reports. Xavier offers him advice about life in France, and about how to make our money go further. They talk about everything. Except 'papers': my father quickly realises that Xavier's had enough of hearing about asylum applications. And our family: Xavier realises even more quickly that it's a subject that's too painful for us. Then it's time to play chess.

'OK Fahim, are you ready?'

I feel a thrill of anticipation. We sit down facing each other across the chessboard. Sometimes Xavier makes me work on my own moves, and sometimes he makes me work on the moves of grandmasters like Garry Kasparov, Anatoly Karpov and Bobby Fischer. We look at them together, do calculations, make up variants. I love thinking up moves, trying them out, advancing, but Xavier makes me slow down a bit:

'Careful now, think. Decide on your goals. What do you want to do: imprison the queen or aim for the king?'

'Um, a bit of both maybe? I dunno, we'll see, whichever's best!'

Then he explains at length why I should take my time. Meanwhile I'm boiling over with impatience.

XP: *Fahim was gifted, no one could doubt that. His tactical skills were outstanding. But as a strategist he was something of a rough diamond. He had no idea about strategy, no conception even of what strategy was. He didn't plan his moves ahead. There was a huge amount of work to do to get him up to standard in this area, so that he could*

91

deploy his talents to the full. As soon as his French was good enough, we got down to it.

Without being a great worker, he was serious, motivated, conscientious and involved. But his progress was held up by his circumstances. In Bangladeshi chess clubs, members play each other every day. In France, they come just for coaching and competitions. People play each other online: the web has killed off the conviviality of clubs. All good players, even the youngest, have a computer. Fahim didn't even have access to the internet.

'Fahim, do you know who said: "To win against me, you have to beat me three times: once in the opening, once in the middlegame and once in the endgame"?'

'It was Alekhine, wasn't it?'

'Precisely so. What you need to do is to work on your endgames. And after that we'll look at your openings.'

'But I'd much rather play whole games!'

'I'm sure you would. I'm not here to "play" with you, though; I'm here to improve your game.'

Sometimes when he isn't looking I watch Xavier. He's the complete opposite of my father. He doesn't care about his appearance, his shirts are all rumpled and his hair is too long – he often forgets to go the barber's. I like it when he has his hair cut and wears a blue shirt that matches his eyes: it makes him look distinguished.

'When it comes to your endgame, Fahim, all you ever do is try to checkmate.'

'Well yes, I want to win, don't I!'

'I can see that: your one aim is to destroy your opponent's king.'

'I want to crush him, massacre him.'

'And yet there are other ways of winning the game. You can win through a promotion, by getting one of your pawns to the opposite side of the board and queening.'

'But while I'm doing that my opponent could checkmate?'

'Of course you need to keep your eye on your opponent! But if you concentrate your efforts on queening, you don't need to go to checkmate: if he's a queen down, your opponent might as well give up there and then.'

'Hey, I like it! Do you think I could do it without my opponent realising?'

Xavier laughs.

'Are there other ways of winning?'

'Over the next few weeks you're going to work on promotion. But you can also immobilise your opponent.'

'One day will you show me how?'

XP: *When he arrived in 2008, Fahim was good enough to win the French under-10s championship with ease. But as he arrived late in the season, he was too late to get his membership card and enter the 2009 championship. We had great hopes for 2010. Then to our huge disappointment we discovered over that winter that the rules required entrants to have lived on French soil for three years. Fahim would have to wait until 2012 to try his chances. To win.*

As Xavier reveals the secrets of the game to me, he also teaches me funny things like the different ways of saying 'checkmate'. When the king is blocked in on the back rank by a row of his own pawns and threatened by a rook, it's called a 'back-rank mate' or 'corridor mate'. When the king can't move because all the squares around him are occupied, it's called 'smothered mate'.

'And when the opposing queen is right up against the king and pinning him down so he can't move?'

'Ah, that's the "kiss of death"!'

While these sessions are going on, my father sits in a corner, silent and discreet. Sometimes he gets up to look at the chessboard and then sits down again. Sometimes he goes off quietly to look round the club and see if there's anything useful he can do. Sometimes he offers 'Exavier' a coffee. Xavier always says yes, and my father rushes off to make it. The last thing he does, every time, is to go outside and spend ages cleaning Xavier's motorbike, as though he wants to get it looking as good as new. It's his way of thanking him for everything: for his coaching sessions, his lessons, his time, his advice, his encouragement, his sympathetic ear, his financial support, his kindness and his cheerfulness. And for his friendship.

Like any teacher, Xavier can be annoying. When he's cross with me he talks, and that's annoying. He does it with the others too. During lessons he sometimes shows one of us up in front of the others. Especially when we haven't done our exercises:

'Don't bother to make excuses. I've heard them all: my sister scratched her foot and the scabs fell in the computer, the anti-virus software had the flu, the cat fell in the washing machine ... I couldn't care less. Everyone's entitled not to do their exercises once or twice in the year. But don't bother telling me why. All I know is that this week doing your exercises wasn't a priority for you.'

Then he often adds:

'But I still like you, even so!'

One day, though, I push him too far:

'I'm sorry Xavier, I haven't done my exercises.'

Exasperated, he shows me the door:

'Goodbye.'

After that I'm always careful to do my exercises.

I can understand why Xavier is fed up when we 'forget' to do the work he sets us, but I can't understand his other obsession, which to me seems very strange: he likes us to be 'punctual'. In Bangladesh no one is ever on time, so no one ever has to wait for anyone else. Xavier just complicates matters by always arriving on time, or even a bit early! He gives me a lecture every time, and sometimes he goes on and on:

'Fahim, this is the third time you've been late for coaching. It's rude. Punctuality is the politeness of kings. Do you think I've got nothing better to do than wait for you to deign to turn up? The next time you're late I'm not going to wait, I warn you.'

I wait politely for the storm to pass. The following week I'm almost on time. Big surprise: the club is shut. At first I think Xavier hasn't arrived yet, and my father and I wait outside in the rain. As it gets later and later, I remember Xavier's threat. I turn to my father:

'*Abba*, do you think Xavier was here and that he left because I was late?'

My father smiles:

'Who put an idea like that in your head? We weren't late. He said five o'clock, and we were here at a quarter past.'

When it starts to get dark, we have to face facts: Xavier isn't here. On the way to the club again a couple of days later, I begin to put on a spurt. I don't like to admit it, but I'm worried: will Xavier be there? From a distance I'm relieved to spot a light in the window. I'm also relieved by the broad grin that greets me as we go in:

'Aha, I see you're on time! Bravo Fahim! I hope Tuesday night has taught you a lesson.'

As it turns out, I'm on time for the rest of the year.

XP: *Some people might have thought I was hard on Fahim. In fact I was more laid back with him than with any of my other pupils, to the extent that sometimes I could feel it gave rise to tensions and jealousies. I made allowances for the ordeals that he'd gone through and the conditions in which he lived. But I train my pupils to win tournaments: they come to me to become champions, not to be babysat.*

97

I can scarcely imagine the great Olympian swimmer Laure Manaudou saying to her trainer: 'I haven't done any swimming this week, I had more important things to do.' Or her trainer replying: 'OK, that's fine by me, see if you can do some next week.'

Fahim's early tournaments brought their fair share of surprises. Some good, some not so good. On the plus side, it turned out that he could play all his moves back from memory, and while this isn't remarkable for a good adult competitive player, for such a young child it's exceptional. It testified to the attitude of a player who seriously wants to improve his game. And to an incredible memory – another of his talents, which took me by surprise on more than one occasion. I remember sending him to a tournament that was being held miles away, near the Gare de l'Est. When I got out the map of the Métro to show him how to get there, he reeled off from memory all the different lines and changes and the names of all the stations along the way: one Sunday when he had nothing else to do he'd learned the map off by heart.

But there were disappointments too. Of course Fahim was a far better player than most of the other under-10s. Against adult opponents he played well, very well even, seeking out their flaws, spotting their mistakes and weaknesses, surprising them and often beating them. But when he played against other children the pace was too slow *for him, and the stakes were too low. He would get bored, slacken off early in the game, let down his guard and then find himself out of his depth. He'd only wake up when disaster was threatening to strike all over the board.*

In April, my friends at the chess club set off for Troyes, for the French championships. Even though I've known for months that I can't compete, and even though I hate travelling, I'm sad to see them go, and a bit angry too. A boy called Chesterkine wins the title. To this day I can't hear his name without bearing him a slight grudge.

'Don't worry, Fahim, I've found you a competition in Paris. The organiser's really nice, you'll see. Over the years he must have spent more time at chess tournaments than Karpov and Kasparov put together.'

Xavier doesn't understand: I couldn't care less about his tournament. I want to compete in the French national championships. And I want to win. Because when I was at the top of the Eiffel Tower I made a promise to myself: one day I'd compete in the European championships. A Bangladeshi at the European championships, now that would be doing it in style! But I don't kid myself: I know my father can't afford to send me there. Not there, not anywhere!

In fact I'll never be able to take part in any international championships – unless I win the French championship first. Then I'll be selected for the French team and the Federation will send me to the European championships. This is my dream, my secret dream. I never tell it to a soul, for fear it might not come true.

Chapter 9

EVERYONE'S CONVINCED

Even Fred's optimistic. The tribunal has sent its report, our application is strong, we're going to get asylum. All the same, Xavier and some of the club members get together to pay for a good lawyer for us. My father is impatient for the hearing. He can't wait to get his 'papers' so he can look for a job and find us somewhere to live. I'm calm and confident: I know everything's going to work out.

XP: *After OFPRA had turned down his application, which was more or less routine, Nura had to lodge an appeal with the Cour Nationale du Droit d'Asile. I was struck from the outset by his confidence, and by that of Frédéric, the social worker at the hostel.*

It was true that France had everything to gain by granting asylum to Fahim. As Jean-Pierre Rosenczveig, president of the children's tribunal at Bobigny, told him with a touch of cynicism:

'If you offer us the prospect of an Olympic medal, even a bronze, but better still a silver or gold, your situation will be regularised within a fortnight. Within a month you will be surprised to discover that your grandfather was French, and afterwards your father as well. Then hot on

their heels, you too will become French. France is prepared to sell her soul for a medal!'

So in order to cover all bases I mobilised the French Chess Federation, which produced a magnificent letter:

'Fahim plays to an exceptional standard, and he is currently the best under-10 player in France. His undeniable contribution can only enhance the reputation of the Federation. Given his level of attainment, it is highly probable that he may represent France at international competitions such as the European and world championships.'

The big day arrives: 21 April 2010. I put on my favourite tracksuit, the white one. My father gets dressed up in his best clothes too. The hearing is in the afternoon. Lots of people come with us: friends from the hostel, both Bangladeshis and others, members of the chess club, Frédéric, Marie-Jeanne and even a director of the French Chess Federation. I didn't know we had so many friends in France.

'Don't worry, Nura, it'll all be fine.'

'With an application like that, what can go wrong?'

'Honestly, it'll be a piece of cake.'

Everyone is smiling. Everyone except my father,

who is overawed. At three o'clock we go into the court-room. Behind a big table sit three judges, two women and a man. I'm surprised, as I thought judges wore robes and wigs, but these ones are in ordinary clothes. A man reads out from a sheet of paper, then our lawyer speaks. Afterwards, the judges ask my father questions and an interpreter translates. When my father doesn't under-stand the question he nods his head, and the judges think he's saying yes. When he understands he answers their questions, describing our life in Bangladesh, talking about me, about chess and tournaments. He gives good answers. I'm glad that no one asks why I was in danger in Dhaka.

At the end, one of the lady judges says we'll be informed of the outcome in three weeks' time. The judges look happy, and so do the lawyer and my father and all our friends. Everyone congratulates my father. In three weeks his name will be posted on the wall, saying 'Asylum granted'. And we'll live in France for ten years, twenty years, maybe for ever. And we can bring over ... but I can't let myself think about that.

Three weeks later, my father and I go back to the tribu-nal. In the Métro he's nervous, and I don't know how to reassure him, so I keep quiet. We get there just as the names are being posted on the walls. We look for my father's name: Asylum granted ... Appeal refused ... Asylum granted ... Appeal refused ... Appeal refused. His name isn't there: not under 'Asylum granted', not under 'Appeal refused'. My father asks me to call our lawyer, who is reassuring:

'The decision's still pending, come back again tomorrow.'

The next day my father gets ready to go back to the tribunal. My friends and I are just beginning a game of football.

'Are you coming, Fahim?'

'We've just started playing! Can you go by yourself?'

'But I can't read French.'

'It's simple: just look for your name with "Asylum granted" beside it.'

My father sighs and sets off, and I go back to playing football.

XP: *The voice on the other end of the phone was unrecognisable. All Nura could say, over and over again, was: 'Exavier, appeal refused, appeal refused ...' He didn't need to understand French to know that in the*

cruel lottery of the asylum-seekers' world he had played and lost.

The man who came to see me at the club early that evening was not the Nura I knew. This was a man who was stunned, overwhelmed by a sense of injustice. His life had just fallen apart, and so had Fahim's.

Refusal by the tribunal was the equivalent of an 'obligation to leave French territory': it meant deportation from France. Nura's situation was now illegal. It was at this point that I began to worry every time he went out, even if he was just going to pick up his son from school at 4:30. I had vivid images imprinted on my mind of an incident outside the primary school on rue Ordener in Montmartre, when parents who were undocumented migrants had been rounded up by the police and taken away.

Paradoxically, this threat didn't apply to Fahim: as a minor, he couldn't be deported. The French authorities could send his father back, and leave him alone in France. I had done some research into what lay in store for unaccompanied child migrants in France. If he was lucky, Fahim would end up in a hostel, which would mean he would have to kiss goodbye to chess, coaching and tournaments. But worse than that, if there was no space in a hostel, he was in danger – like many other child migrants – of ending up on the streets, forced to queue up every night to beg for a bed from humanitarian organisations who are obliged by lack of funds to select those young people who are most at risk. I'd heard someone who worked with these children describing how one winter's night the only thing he'd been able to offer a child who was sleeping rough was a sleeping bag.

Later on, Fahim would be able to apply for asylum or a residence permit. I could imagine only too easily what would happen next, with his identity, date of birth and age all potentially called into question. Because the French authorities would undoubtedly try to deport him, and they would want to establish how soon they could do so. Even before his eighteenth birthday, they would demand a judicial medical assessment: an obsolete test of his bones, a dental examination (an echo of the slave trade in its heyday), and a humiliating assessment of his genitals and body hair.

Although they were not yet at that stage, for Nura and Fahim a life on the streets now beckoned. France Terre d'Asile was financed by the public purse, and so could only offer accommodation to asylum-seekers. Now that their application had been turned down, father and son would have to leave the hostel and make way for new applicants. Fortunately the hostel staff were humane. They had been touched by Fahim and Nura's story, and had become particularly involved in their application. So they put off the inevitable for as long as they could, and turned

to the network of local charities to try to find alternative
accommodation for them.

Since the tribunal handed down its verdict, my father
has been silent, worried, serious. He spends ages staring
into empty space, and when we eat in the evening he
forgets to talk to me. I don't know what to say to make
him feel better. He doesn't react even when I tell him
I'm going to be put up a class at school. But at the Paris
championships in the early summer I manage to squeeze
a smile out of him: I've made so much progress with
my endgames that I win the tournament, playing against
adults, and when I give him the first prize of 1,000 euros
my father looks relieved.

XP: *During this tournament, a 'guru' figure circled around*
Fahim. The unconventional methods espoused by this 'tel-
evangelist of Parisian chess' (of necessity, as he barely
knew how to play) were exemplary. He would teach begin-
ners himself, but for the most promising pupils he would
recruit masters and grandmasters from abroad, exploiting
them like a slave driver. When the truth about his methods

dawned on them, he would send them home and import others.

Dressed up to look rather like Desmond Tutu, he would target relatives who were loaded with wealth (he would run a practised eye over the old biddies' jewellery as he set his highly flexible rates) and with ambition, and who fondly imagined that their children were more intelligent than their peers. I even heard that he had managed to persuade one credulous grandmother to buy a 'life membership' for her grandson, who inevitably gave up chess soon afterwards.

This 'guru' had a nose for sniffing out gifted players, and a talent for exploiting their prowess while convincing the world that it was all down to his teaching methods. So he hovered over Fahim, before offering money to Nura to sign him up for his club. When Nura – who doubtless had some experience of dealing with crooks and swindlers – mockingly suggested that he should ask me direct, his expression was a sight to behold.

In the summer, my friends in the club set off to play in the tournament at Saint-Affrique in the Aveyron. I'm envious of them, but travelling around is expensive. I have to stay behind on my own with Xavier at Marie-Jeanne's house, and I get a bit bored. I spend a lot of time on the internet, playing chess and going on journeys on Google and YouTube.

On 26 July it's my tenth birthday. I'm sad: now I'll never be the French under-10s champion.

'Xavier, did Einstein really say that "Chess players ruin their lives instead of doing important things"?'

'He was talking about his friend Emmanuel Lasker, world chess champion, and what he actually said was: "The strong chess player is a man endowed with a brain of extraordinary abilities which he squanders fruitlessly at a chessboard instead of using them for far more important ends." Was he right, do you think?'

'No!'

'Then hang on to this quotation from Tarrasch instead: "I have always had a slight feeling of pity for the man who has no knowledge of chess, just as I would for a man who is ignorant of love. Chess, like love, like music, has the power to make men happy."'

I play in the Plancoët tournament, and for the first time in my life I play against an international master, the Bulgarian player Velislav Kukov. Sitting opposite him is exciting: I so badly want to beat him. At the start of the game he takes the advantage. I try to catch up. Too late. I'm caught in Kukov's traps. I try to hold on. Help! All I can do is counter his attacks. Then suddenly inside my head I hear Xavier saying: 'Don't let your opponent lead you by the nose. A good player doesn't think much of what his opponent does, despises it even. That's why many people think chess players are conceited.'

This gets a reaction from me, just as Kukov starts to slow down. He probably thinks I'm just a kid who doesn't know how to follow up my moves. You have no idea who you're up against, pal! He exchanges queens? Excellent! Exactly what I was counting on. Now I decide to go for promotion: I advance, I roll forward, I flood him with a wave of pawns. He refuses to sacrifice a bishop, and his rook falls into my trap. I send a pawn on ahead to release my queen. He spots his mistake. Too late! My first victory against a master. He's so annoyed that he flings his score sheet across the board. I'm jubilant. Next day, Xavier shows me an article with my photo in a newspaper called *Ouest-France*. It's a shame my father can't read French.

XP: *The win against Kukov – doubtless helped (being realistic) by the fact that the master was exhausted after a long*

journey – was the culmination of good steady progress on Fahim's part. He had listened to advice, put his coaching into practice, made a plan in his head, established a goal, put it into effect, and caught out a master. The young and gifted competitor was turning into a true player.

This achievement also marked the end of an era. Fahim never spoke of his personal circumstances now. Whenever I talked to his father about such matters he would stand a little way off or look at something else, as if all the problems they faced didn't concern him. While everyone else was devastated by the tribunal's decision, he carried on looking as unconcerned as ever. Some people thought he was oblivious. And yet, this boy who was usually so composed now looked nervous in tournaments and couldn't stop fidgeting. Already that spring, a championship final had shone a clear light on his state of mind. In a game that he had planned carefully both tactically and strategically, he was well ahead both in time – meaning his opponent had to play faster – and in position. He had seized control of all the white squares, so confining his opponent to the black squares, and he was fighting him for those every inch of the way. All of a sudden, when the game was virtually his, Fahim let a key defensive pawn go on the attack, opening up the field for his opponent. 'Impatience in small things confounds great projects,' as Confucius said. With a single move, he lost the game.

I didn't yet know it, but Fahim was about to be sucked into the depths of a dark vortex. Just as he was learning how to view his game strategically, he was overtaken by events. The boy who had loved the fight, the tension, the tactics and clever moves, now charged headfirst into the fray, preferring speed and bluff to reflection, not bothering to project into the future, trying to knock his opponent off balance through his sheer nerve, as though he was driven by an overwhelming secret rage. This boldness and daring would come into their own at fast-paced blitz games, but during slow games they could get him into trouble, and increasingly into danger.

After the holidays in Brittany I go back to Créteil – in time to pack my bags. We gather our things together and leave them at the chess club, which isn't used during the summer. I leave my trophies behind in Muhamad's office, where he will keep them safe. The twelfth of August is heartbreaking. We walk out of the hostel, leaving behind us our friends and playmates, our sense of security and our hopes, and eighteen months of peaceful and almost normal life. We go to a small hotel on the other side of Créteil where the hostel staff have hassled the emergency helpline for homeless people into finding us a room. It's clean and nice, but sad. When I open the window, the room is filled with the smell of the McDonald's next door.

As soon as we get there, I search my bags for my coin collection: euros, centimes, Arabic coins and loads of others from places I don't know, that I've found on the ground or people have given me. Coins that I've kept in case one day I might need them. A secret treasure store that I keep in a red tin that my father brought home. I've stuck labels with the days of the week inside it. I've put each coin in the section matching the day when I found it, and all the sections are full. I haven't shown my treasure to anyone, not even my friends. I get it out when I'm on my own, and it reassures me, makes me feel I'm rich. It was the first thing I got ready to put in my case. But I look everywhere and I can't find it: it isn't there. I can feel the rage rising inside me, rage at this life that's taken away from me everything I have.

Chapter 10

LIFE ON HOLD

Usually I like going back to school at the start of the year – for a day or so anyway – but this year I drag my feet all the way. Nothing's how it used to be: my gang have made new friends, kids who've arrived at the hostel over the summer, and I feel left out. After school my father and I go to the hostel, where Yolande is waiting to help me with my homework. Everyone is very nice to us. While I do my school work, my father finds a little corner in one of the kitchens and makes us a hot meal: no sandwiches for us tonight. Then we go back to the hotel, where I let the time drift past, watch cartoons and go to bed to forget.

Every other week, we have to phone the homeless emergency helpline. Since my father doesn't speak very good French, I make the call for him. I feel awkward, uncomfortable, embarrassed by the feeling that we're begging. When I pick up the phone I have a hollow feeling in my stomach: please let them say we can stay where we are. My father watches me intently, listening, studying my responses, straining to understand. Everything depends on me, as if I'm the adult and he's the child. It weighs on me so much that sometimes I hang up and don't say anything, don't tell him what the answer was. Then instantly I feel sorry and I'm really nice to him again.

We get another fortnight! Once, twice, three times!

Then they're going to do building work, so one day we have to leave and go to another hotel. Fortunately the helpline people manage to find us a room in a nearby town called Bonneuil. We pack our bags and move on again. And every fortnight I call again.

Then we have to leave the second hotel, only this time the helpline can't find us anywhere else to go. There's no space anywhere. So I call back again, and again and again, until in the end they find us a room in Paris. Miles away. I write down the address on a scrap of paper, find it on a Métro map and explain to my father. We get moved on from one hotel to another, each of them worse than the one before, until one evening we find ourselves in a real hovel, a tiny, filthy broom cupboard at the end of a dark corridor, with toilets that are unusable and washing facilities on another floor. I didn't know it was possible for anything to be so filthy. We cling on to the room even so, and I make my fortnightly calls over and over and over again: please let us stay here, please, please let us live here!

My father wakes me up early. Exhausted, I catch the Métro for the journey to school in Créteil, which seems to go on for ever. At first Céline, my teacher, asks me why I look so tired, why I don't pay attention. I'm too ashamed to tell her the truth, so I say I stayed up late watching television. But after a few days she stops asking, and when she goes round the class and between the rows of desks she sometimes puts her hand on my shoulder. After school my father takes me to the hostel or the chess club, then we set off on the journey 'home'. Weekends are yet another round of endless journeys, to lessons, coaching and tournaments. I can't cope with it any more. I fall asleep on the Métro. I fall asleep when we're eating. I fall asleep at school. And when I play chess I rock to and fro all the time, like a robot with no off switch.

Then one day my father snaps, not for himself, but for me. He asks me to call the helpline and describe how we're being forced to live. To tell them. To beg them. At the other end of the line I can hear people talking. They sound embarrassed. Finally they find us a hotel in Saint-Maur, next door to Créteil. So we go back to Val-de-Marne and to a gentler pace of life. I go to bed earlier, get up later, go to school by bus, get my breath back. And I try to get rid of the black moths that are always fluttering about inside my head.

On my father's furrowed brow, worries pile up like storm clouds. We've run out of money. At the hostel we were given 285 euros a month to buy food, clothes and other essentials. It wasn't much and we had to economise, but we managed. My father used even to set aside 30 euros each month for the time when we would leave the hostel and move into our own home. He would get cross if I wasted money. Like the time when I was playing with my friends on a hill, and the room key fell out of my pocket. I went back over my steps and looked everywhere, but I couldn't find it. My father lost his temper and shouted at me: having another key cut would cost 50 euros. Then he went round with that scary expression all day. After that I was more careful.

Now he gets nothing. The 1,000 euros from the Paris championship has gone. Our pockets are empty. Some nights we have nothing to eat. Sometimes I think I'm going to die of hunger. Fortunately Xavier is there, always generous when we need to eat, buy trainers for school or pay entrance fees for tournaments.

XP: *Fahim and Nura spoke little about their problems: so little that not everyone around them was aware of their situation. Some people, naturally mindful of others and generous in their response, were always there for them, offering both financial and moral support. Not everyone though. One night I remember losing my temper*

with families at the club who would reel off all the usual clichés about 'feckless' foreigners who 'weren't capable of bringing up children'. Thinking of Nura, I told them how much respect these parents deserved – parents who were prepared to sacrifice their own wellbeing for the sake of their children's future, men and women capable of travelling halfway round the world to ensure their children's safety. Blinded by their prejudices, some of these people at the club hadn't noticed a thing, and they were knocked sideways. I turned to one of the boys:

'You remember last week, when the heating at the club was on the blink?'

'You told us to put our jumpers on.'

'Do you remember what Fahim said?'

'Yes, he said he didn't have a jumper.'

'Did you understand what he meant by that?'

'Well yeah, he'd left it at home.'

'No. When Fahim said he didn't have a jumper, he meant that he didn't have a jumper.'

There was silence. The next week, the same boy arrived with a bundle of clothes for Fahim and Nura. At that point I think some of them began to open their eyes.

Without a visa, my father isn't allowed to work. For a

long time he has respected this ban, because he doesn't want to be in a position that's illegal. But he thinks it's cruel that he isn't able to make himself useful. So he helps out in any way he can. Rather than hanging around all day doing nothing, he does the cleaning at the chess club and a bit of gardening for Marie-Jeanne in Brittany, and he helps out at the hostel at short notice whenever the staff need it. It's his way of saying thank you to all the people who have helped us.

He's got into the habit of combing the streets to salvage anything that people have thrown away and that can still be used: televisions, microwaves, children's clothes, crockery and so on. He takes it all back to the hostel and gives it to people who've just arrived and who have nothing.

Then my sister Jhorna becomes very ill. She has water on the brain and constant nosebleeds. She needs an emergency operation, but in Bangladesh there's no social security: if the family can't pay for the operation and hospital care, then the sick person stays at home. And they die.

My father is desperate. We don't have a penny, and he needs to find 1,500 euros, urgently. Swallowing his shame at being forced to beg, he turns once again to Xavier, who – as always – comes to his aid. It isn't enough, though. One of Xavier's friends who we don't even know pays the rest, and then a chess player offers my father a job helping him to re-lay his floor. For the first time in a long while, I see my father smile. He is taking control of our lives again. Jhorna has the operation and it saves her life.

XP: *After this experience, Nura decided to defy the ban and carry on working. He couldn't bear to be a burden on society any longer. From then on he searched everywhere, asked everyone, thought of every job imaginable. I lost count of the times he arrived at the club triumphantly brandishing one of those free newspapers, in which he'd circled lucrative-looking small ads promising 'Top deals', 'Win 2,000 euros a month', 'Set up your own business'. Every time I had to be a wet blanket, warning him off cons and fraudsters.*

He got it into his head that he was going to sell fruit in the Métro, but soon had to give up that idea. To get a contract with RATP, the transport operator, he would need a valid work permit. He thought he could use me as his front man, and it was only with the greatest difficulty that I managed to convince him of the risks that we would both be running.

On another occasion he got wind of a small business

selling mobile phones. I had to explain to him that this would undoubtedly be merchandise that had 'fallen off the back of a lorry'.

But I did lend him the money to buy a Chinese trader's stock of wallets, belts, hats, gloves, necklaces and miniature Eiffel Towers, and at the weekend he would set up a makeshift stall in the market at Montreuil. That brought him in a little money, until the police arrived and confiscated his stock, along with that of a lot of other minor street traders. He left with 10 euros in his pocket, upset but pleasantly surprised by the courteousness of the police officers, and relieved not to have been taken away by them.

Nura was an excellent handyman, and for a while he worked cash-in-hand as a painter on building sites, where he was greatly valued by his bosses for his efficient work and conscientious attitude. But his early positive experiences were soon followed by other less happy ones, such as the building site where he had to wait two months to be paid, the one where he was paid 150 euros for 75 hours' work (or 2 euros an hour), and the one where after two weeks the foreman in charge claimed not to know who he was and sent him packing empty-handed. So then he decided not to work any more for people he didn't know. But his lack of French narrowed down the possibilities. He couldn't be taken on as the duty volunteer at the chess club, for instance, because he was unable to welcome visitors and answer their questions. Fortunately, tournaments were an opportunity to make new contacts. Some parents asked him to give chess lessons to their son in the afternoons. Fahim would go with him as interpreter. The journeys were time-consuming and meant that Fahim had to miss his own lessons. Nura stopped doing it.

The same concerns about location stopped him from taking up a job as full-time carer to a very old lady who lived on the outskirts of the Paris area. It was too far from Créteil for Fahim to be able to come to coaching more than occasionally. Nura was prepared to sacrifice everything for a job and a normal life: everything except his son.

His limited grasp of French was a source of daily frustration for Nura. Months after the event, he told me rather sheepishly – though he could also see its funny side – about an incident that had nearly tipped over into farce. After going to have his hair cut in the Belleville district, he had gone into a café to use the toilet. While he was waiting, a young Asian girl came up and started talking to him. He could make out the words 'work' and '40 euros'. Delighted at having found a job, or so he thought, he followed her back to her place. No sooner had they gone inside than she took all her clothes off and demanded 40 euros.

Dumbfounded, Nura grasped the nature of the transaction and fled, while she yelled after him, calling him all the names under the sun.

Not all of Nura's adventures were so entertaining: far from it, in fact. Through the experiences he confided in me, I learned about the world of those with no money, no documentation, no defences and no rights. As he was coming out of the Métro one evening, a man set upon him for no reason and started beating him up. He punched Nura to the ground, then attacked him with a volley of kicks. When a police car came around the corner, the attacker took fright and ran off. Their suspicions aroused, the police officers stopped the car and came over to Nura:

'What's going on here? Why were you fighting with that man?'

'No worry, no worry,' replied Nura, struggling to his feet with difficulty.

Then a bystander intervened:

'I saw it all: this gentleman was coming out of the Métro minding his own business when the other man launched an unprovoked attack on him.'

The police officers' attitude softened:

'Are you all right, sir? Are you hurt?'

'OK, no worry,' protested Nura, terrified that they might ask him for his papers.

'Would you like us to take you to hospital?'

'No, no! All fine,' he repeated, panic-stricken.

'Come with us to the police station to make a statement.'

'No, no! No problem. Much much no problem.'

'But you need to stand up for yourself. Come with us.'

'No, no! No problem, no worry.'

Nura was on the verge of tears. So plaintive were his pleas that the police officers let him go. He staggered painfully back to the hotel. The next day he had to drag himself to the nearest accident and emergency department.

I don't know why, but for a while I've been going through a bad phase. I keep losing, even against weak players. At one tournament, I'm flattened in 30 moves. My opponent takes one of my pawns and attacks the rampart that I've built around my king. As he does it I just watch: I can't react, can't defend myself. When it gets to checkmate, it's all I can do to stop myself from crying.

My father is furious. He flies into a terrible temper and won't speak to me for two days. He doesn't speak to me in the morning. He doesn't speak to me on the way to school. He doesn't speak to me on the way back from school. He doesn't speak to me when we eat. He just says nothing, as if I'm not there. He won't do anything for me. He doesn't even wash up my plate after supper. So I wait for him to speak to me. I know he will. He'll have to, he needs me to translate. But it goes on for ever and it hurts.

Another time, he looks on as the game I'm playing collapses. I can feel him getting crosser and crosser. Soon all I can think about is how angry he is, I can't think about the game at all. When the tournament is over, he picks up his things and leaves. I run after him, down the street, into the Métro. When we get to the hotel he won't speak. I feel so bad.

I refuse to eat and go and sulk in front of the television. Luckily I find a packet of crisps in my pocket, a bet I won off a friend at the club. I eat them in silence and manage to make my father feel guilty. I'm not proud of myself, though.

Sometimes I overhear conversations between parents at the club without them realising. They say that it's no good for a child to live like this, and that I'm disturbed by what's happening to me. That annoys me, as they seem to be criticising my father and to think that the situation is his fault. And above all because I'm not disturbed, I refuse to be disturbed. In my head I want to be strong.

XP: *While all this was going on, I went on the offensive with the Federation to get them to allow Fahim to compete in the French championship. It put my relationship with them under some strain: this was time spent in the wilderness for someone as outspoken as me, who knows that people don't always want to hear the truth but prefers to tell it anyway. Behind the scenes, I put pressure on my contacts to change the rules and bring them into line with those of the major sports federations. The idea was picked up and championed by other people who had no idea where it came from. The championships were now opened up to all foreign children who were in full-time education in France, as long as they had a licence that had to be obtained at the beginning of the season.*

The news brought a smile to Fahim's face, even though lack of funds meant that he rarely took part in tournaments outside the Paris region. But the turn for the worse that he'd taken in the spring had become even more worrying by the autumn. He seemed to have lost his appetite for chess completely. When he sat down at the chessboard his eyes had lost their sparkle. He was half-hearted in lessons, at tournaments he just slumped in his chair, and his remarkable memory was losing its power. After one lost game, I looked at his score sheet and felt bewildered. Where was the Fahim I knew, the clever, agile rascal, the rebel fired up with reckless enthusiasm? After the opening, instead of sending his troops into battle he had retreated in order to defend a pawn that was of no importance. The victim of circumstances beyond his control, he avoided confrontation and withdrew anxiously into his own camp. He seemed to have lost all the fighting spirit that had been so much a part of him and had enabled him to reach his full potential. He was losing even that most fundamental attribute of a good player: his confidence in himself. He was becoming a timid and anxious opponent, who could work out his moves but had lost his dynamism. During coaching and at lessons, I would resort to every subterfuge – using provocation and humour on top of my teaching skills – in my attempts to reawaken the champion in him.

One evening when we're playing, Xavier attacks and forces me to retreat. He frowns:

'Fahim, the Russians never retreat!'

'Why do you say that?'

'It's a famous story about a Russian master who lost to a lower-ranking player by letting him capture his knight rather than retreating.'

'That wasn't clever, he lost!'

'He lost that game, admittedly. But he was playing 30 opponents at once. And through his refusal to retreat he won the other 29. The Russians are great attackers. Take them as an example, adopt an attacking style. Never retreat and you'll win most of your games.'

'But I'm not a Russian,' I shrug. Xavier doesn't like it when I shrug.

'True, you're not a Russian. But in chess the Russians are the best, so take them as your example.'

'I don't like the Russians. I prefer the Napoleons!'

'The who?'

'The Napoleons. I learned about them at school: the Napoleons attacked the Russians.'

Xavier smiles.

'And then what happened?'

'I don't know.'

'Didn't your teacher tell you what happened when Napoleon's troops retreated?'

'Um ...'

'The Battle of Berezina.'

'The what?'

'The Battle of Berezina.'

Xavier tells me a tale of a frozen river, melting ice, drowned regiments and disaster. It's fascinating. Then we start playing again. I am the Napoleons and Xavier is the Russians:

'Look Fahim! The Russians never retreat!'

I refuse to give up any squares:

'Nor do the Napoleons!'

After that game it becomes a sort of catchphrase for us:

'The Russians never retreat!'

'Nor do the Napoleons!'

At a tournament a few months later, I handle the opening well but then find myself plunged into the unknown. My opponent is pushing me into a corner but I refuse to retreat. In a sudden burst of arrogance, I launch a counter-attack, Russian-style.

'It is at the moment of death that a chess player clings on to life,' as Alekhine would say.

I refuse to give in, and soon my opponent is sweating like mad. He's doing any old thing, and then he collapses. Phew! I've won! At last!

XP: *Despite a few good games, Fahim wasn't on the right wavelength for chess any more. 'You can't look up at the stars when you have a stone in your shoe.' I wasn't sure what to do, whether to give him some breathing space or to push him? But the one thing I know how to do is to be a trainer. Forcing him to get a grip, encouraging him always to do better was my way of supporting him so that he could keep his head above water. And on top of this I also had*

the feeling that somehow – even if I couldn't see quite how exactly – chess could be a lifeline for him and his father.

At the time I put the emphasis on chess as a sport. I know it's an idea that tends to raise a smile, but chess – sitting as it does at the interface of games, science and culture – is also a sport. In France it falls under the remit of the Ministry of Sport, moreover. To play chess you need to be fit both physically and mentally and to train regularly. Chess tournaments work like other sports competitions, with championships, rankings, trainers and referees. And if anyone objects that it's not very physical, I would remind them that rifle shooting from a prone position is an Olympic discipline. And I'd add that, like footballers and tennis players, great chess players give up competitive playing around the age of 40, rather than struggling to continue to play at an international level.

With Fahim, therefore, I insisted that he should adopt the regime of an athlete, with plenty of sleep (even if a healthy diet wasn't always possible) and a competitive stance: not slumped in his chair, but upright, chest out and arms crossed on the table to make his presence felt to his opponent. I hoped this would help him to rediscover the dynamic of the game, his will to attack and his will to win. His will to play.

That winter I go on the school ski trip. Since I don't have any skiing kit, everyone chips in, at school, at the club and at the hostel. In the end, by the time we set off my bag is the biggest of all of them. It's a long journey. The peculiar smell in the train carriage gives me a headache. It's like being in a car, only with a different smell. Every journey is a bad memory.

It's late in the evening when we get to the chalet. In our room we laugh and shout and make a noise late into the night. The others can't sleep and Céline tells us off.

In the morning, some of the others sail effortlessly down the pistes, while I manage to get my skis on and try to look as if I know what I'm doing. But my feet slip from under me, my legs fly off in all directions and there's no way I can stay upright. Luckily the others in my group are just as bad, and we all take turns to fall flat on our faces. I can't stop laughing, especially when a boy I can't stand comes over and tries to act all cool but ends up in a heap at my feet. When it comes to my turn to show what I can do I really try hard: the instructor is nice and I want to impress her. I quickly change my mind about snow and fix on a goal: I'm going to go back with my *flocon*, my first ski qualification.

At the end of the trip I don't want to leave – unlike some of the others, who've cried all the time as they're so desperate to see their mothers again. I never cry about my mother, even when I'm feeling really miserable because I miss her so much. There's no point: it won't make her suddenly appear. But God knows how much I want to see her, to tell her about everything. About skiing. About tournaments. About all the rest. I imagine her putting her arms around me and telling me I've done well.

Sometimes we talk on the phone, always in a rush, with just time to say:

'How are you?'

'Where are you?'

'Are you eating properly?'

'Are you sleeping well?'

Sometimes she passes the phone to Jhorna or Fahad so that I can hear their voices. We tell each other we're fine. And that's it. Jhorna and I are like strangers now. And I don't know Fahad at all. When I left he was still a baby and slept all the time. I don't know anything about him. Who is he? What does he think about? What does he dream about? And what does he make of this big brother who he's never seen?

The telephone is a link that tells us that we're all still alive. Every time, my mother starts to cry and I cut the call short and hang up. I tell myself it's because calls are expensive.

Letters are another link. I can still read Bengali, but I

can't write it any more. So I make do with reading the letters my mother sends, letters in which she says the same things over and over again: I'm well, everything's fine, everyone's well, you mustn't worry about us, eat properly my son, sleep well, look after yourself. She doesn't tell us that she's run out of money, that she's in debt, that she's moved a long way out of the centre of Dhaka. She just says that everything's fine. And I believe her.

For a while now these links have been broken. My father doesn't show me her letters any more and stops calling her when I'm there. He can see it's too painful for me. And I've started to forget her face. When I'm alone I concentrate hard and try to picture her, but she's gone. I don't even have any photos to help call back her memory.

Sometimes I blame my father for taking me so far away from my mother. I blame my mother for letting me go. But mostly I blame myself. Everything that's happened is my fault: if I hadn't loved chess so much my father wouldn't have been forced to take me and run away.

Then I dream that I raise a regiment to fight the bad people who forced us to leave. I conquer India with a small force, then with a more powerful army I conquer the whole of Asia, then Europe and last of all China, because there are so many people in China. With all the people of Asia and Europe and China behind me, I confront my enemies. I make them take off their black masks and show their faces. I threaten them the way they threatened me. But I wouldn't hurt their wives. Or their children.

Then I become president, and there is a statue of me at the North Pole with the inscription 'FAHIM THE KING'. I build an enormous palace of gold and diamonds. I set off with my army to fetch my family, and when I find my mother ...

The ski trip is over. The journey back takes ages. The others are impatient to get home. I'm just scared. What if my father hasn't managed to phone the helpline? What if they've made us move to a different hotel? What if my father doesn't come to collect me? What if I never find him again?

Luckily he's there to meet me. But after that I'm always afraid of losing him. Of losing him as well.

XP: *After the tribunal's decision, Nura explored every avenue and exhausted every possibility for staying in*

France, trying to obtain a family residence permit and then a work residence permit, and trailing from the Préfecture at Créteil to the administrative tribunal at Melun, the administrative court of appeal in Paris, and back again.

He had worked out that this was an area in which I was incapable of offering him any effective help: I often say that in life I can only count up to eight and read up to the letter H – just enough to identify the squares on a chessboard. Luckily he found a valuable source of help in Hélène, president of the chess club and a petite bundle of energy. You couldn't help but admire their tenacity and determination. At every step of the way new obstacles were thrown in their path: making appointments, collecting files, filling in forms, filling in more forms because they'd changed colour, writing letters, telling their story, proving they had integrated, demonstrating how hard Fahim was working at school, showing his good results and his successes at chess, and sending for documents from Bangladesh and having them photocopied and translated, with all the expenditure this implied in terms of both energy and money.

Each new attempt was met with refusal and ended with a new order to leave French soil. The responses of the authorities were Kafkaesque. At different times, Nura was told to supply a long-stay visa, proof of his address, a statement of child allowance payments and even pay slips – all of which he didn't have precisely because of his irregular position in France. And how many times was he asked, above all, to supply proof of the threats to which Fahim had been subject in Bangladesh? How he regretted not having kept that anonymous letter that he had received in Bangladesh!

On several occasions their file was lost. In Bangladesh, civil status consists only of two forenames, with no family name. Which of these two names should be used as identification, the first or the second? Following an ingenious combination of the forenames of Fahim and Nura in the national register of aliens – to which only the bureaucrats held the key – their file was lost for ever. So they had to go back to the beginning again.

As one rejection followed another, so Nura underwent a great change. He never smiled any more, and his complexion faded from its handsome warm tone to a dull grey. The man who had been preoccupied but active now sank deeper into depression with each passing day. Helpless, overwhelmed, broken and close to being destroyed, he was crumbling away. In his place he was leaving a ghost.

My father still believes in miracles. He sees a television commercial: 'To know your future, call our clairvoyant on 0800 ...' He wants me to make the call. I try to dissuade him, but nothing will change his mind: he wants to know if we'll get our visas soon. I dial the number and wait, and wait. After many long minutes the line goes dead. The credit on his mobile has run out. Our answer will have to wait for another day.

XP: *In 2011, the Ministry of the Interior announced that henceforth France considered Bangladesh as a safe country. The thousands of Bangladeshi nationals living in France, who at that time made up the largest number of asylum-seekers, could go home. This bore little relation to the realities of life in Bangladesh as depicted in the press. Even OFPRA, the government agency with responsibility for refugees, cited in a report the continuing violence and insecurity there, describing the democratic process as fragile. The damage was done, alas, and the authorities refused to budge: Nura would have to go.*

The small world of chess, which was becoming quite experienced in such matters, was now to demonstrate once again its capacity for mobilisation and solidarity. There are many trainers who get involved on a daily basis in order to help pupils who are in difficulties, whether on a psychological or a social level. Lots of them give lessons to undocumented immigrants, not knowing whether these pupils – Chechen or Kosovar, Armenian or Sri Lankan – will still be here the next school year, or even the next week. In 2011, the club in Maisons-Altfort, next door to Créteil, mobilised in support of a young Nicaraguan boy who had lived in France for ten years. He had arrived with his mother who had married a Frenchman – who treated him and loved him as his own son – and he lived with them and the two children they had together. As soon as he reached the age of eighteen, he was to be deported from France and sent to Nicaragua, where he knew no one. But through their actions the club members succeeded in getting him freed on the tarmac, just minutes before the plane was due to take off.

Elsewhere, the father of a former pupil of mine found himself in the front line in the affair of Blendi and Blendon, twins whose parents had fled with them to safety from Kosovo. Blendon had suffered a brain haemorrhage that had left him paralysed down one side. He and his family were deported to Kosovo just before he was due to have the operation that might have restored much of his mobility.

That same day, France was condemned by the European Court of Human Rights for the inhumane and degrading treatment it inflicted on children placed in detention centres, citing notably a baby that had been deprived of milk for many hours.

These stories made it all too clear that for Fahim – who had no home, no papers, no money and nothing resembling the stable and dignified life to which every child has a right – there were yet further depths to which he could sink. To which he was about to sink.

Chapter 11

CASTLES IN SPAIN

As soon as my name is put down for the French championships I begin to feel there's hope again. So much so that when Hélène, the club president, says to me in January, '2011 will be your year', I want to believe her. I have a feeling that my dream's about to come true at last.

But in fact 2011 will turn out to be the worst year of my life.

XP: *The French youth championships, held in April every year, attract hundreds of young players – boys and girls aged from six to twenty – from throughout France and the French overseas territories. The heats are divided into sections according to age, and there are nine rounds spread over eight days: one round per day for eight days, with two rounds on the ninth. A game lasts three to four hours, or sometimes even more. To win, a player must checkmate his or her opponent (which is rare), force them to resign (when the game is so uneven that there is no point in going on), or let them time out (if they're close to running out of time). Occasionally games end in a draw.*

I put on a brave face for the journey to Montluçon, which is really long. When we get there, I go to find the accommodation that the club is renting, explore the Centre Athanor where the competition will be held, and race out on to the pitch behind the competition halls to kick a ball about.

Before and after our chess games, we charge outside to play endless games of football. I know some of the players who come from the Paris region, and some from the provinces because I've met them before at the team championships. Now I get to know more of them, including a boy called Théo, who's good fun, says hello to everyone and shares his sweets. Soon I discover his one flaw: whenever he loses, either at football or at chess, he goes crazy. At first I'm surprised, but after a while I just think it's funny.

XP: *The chess championships are a world unto themselves. Or rather two worlds: the world of the competitors in the competition halls, and the world of their families and trainers outside.*

The atmosphere in the playing area is like a study room at a boarding school: nobody says a word, but there's a buzz in the air. Against a background of tension and the ticking of clocks, the ambience goes through different phases: in the initial stages of the games the moves come quickly; then, as the problems become more complex and the ranks of the competitors are thinned as more and more of them are knocked out, the pace slows down.

The players move about a lot: at this age especially it's impossible to stay sitting still for hours at a time without losing your concentration. On the contrary, you have to keep getting up, moving around, unwinding, discreetly letting off steam, giving vent to rage or despair, or simply getting a change of air or perspective. So while half the players consider their next move, their opponents stretch their legs, go off to get a drink at the far end of the hall, go to the toilet or watch a different game.

The boys are livelier, the girls quieter. The younger girls line their lucky mascots up beside the chessboard, while the older ones are chic and carefully groomed; the rooms where the boys play, on the other hand, smell of sweat and trainers. Some of the boys are obviously nervous, tipping their chairs back, swinging their legs and drumming their fingers. Others are still as statues, staring into space, apparently daydreaming or even nodding off. But in fact all of them are on high alert.

Outside, the atmosphere is charged. For friends and supporters, club presidents, trainers and above all the players' parents and families, the hours of waiting are tense and anxious. It's like a school sports day: everyone's in competition, everyone's in the same boat. People drink coffee and watch the games live-streamed on the internet. Whenever the door opens they turn round to look. Immediately they can tell what's happened: the player coming out will either be king of the world or wrung out, exhausted, pale and shattered. Garry Kasparov described chess as 'the most violent sport there is'. As a mental fight to the death, chess is far more brutal than most martial arts. Victory is a triumph; defeat is correspondingly agonising, comfortless and lonely.

For me these are happy days, with nothing to worry about, no emergency helpline to call, no homework to do, no chess exercises even. Nothing but playing chess and enjoying life: a week of battles on the chessboard and having fun with friends. And with Xavier. With Xavier there's no way you could ever be bored, he always has so many ideas for games to play, and such a fund of stories to tell and songs to sing. We'll ask him if he knows a song with a particular word in it – 'window', or 'table', say – and however hard we try to trap him he can always think of something.

At Montluçon Xavier is on outstanding form. As

soon as we get there he plays us a track by a band called Mickey 3D which is quite rude about Montluçon, and we all end up singing it the whole time.

'Xavier, tell us the story of Nimzowitsch and the cigar.'

'At a tournament, Nimzowitsch's opponent rested a cigar on the edge of the chessboard. Nimzowitsch, who detested the smell of tobacco, demanded that the referee should enforce the ban on smoking. The player with the cigar protested that he hadn't lit the cigar and therefore wasn't smoking, and the referee was forced to concede that he was in the right. Whereupon Nimzowitsch retorted: "You know very well that in chess the threat is more powerful than its execution!" And it's true, a single piece may pose several different threats at once. But as soon as it moves to put one of these threats into practice, it cancels out all the others. For Nimzowitsch, life and chess obeyed the same rules.'

At mealtimes, Xavier thinks of a word and we have to guess its meaning. I learn a whole range of obscure words including 'fulminate', 'procrastinate' (I have no trouble understanding what that means), 'carminative' (which sends Loulou into fits of giggles), 'saxicolous' and 'catadioptric'. I also learn the word *épectase*, or 'orgasm', but I'm not sure I understand what it means. Xavier tells a story about a French president who died of *une épectase* while he was with his mistress. The grown-ups all scream with laughter, especially when Xavier reaches the punchline:

'When the doctor arrived he asked: "*Le président a-t-il encore sa connaissance?*" ("Is the president still conscious?"). And the guard on duty (understanding the other possible meaning, "Is the president's lady friend still with him?") replied: "No, she left by the service stairs."'

'Xavier, couldn't you think of a different word?', asks Hélène. 'Think of the children!'

'But,' protests Xavier, all innocence, 'it's history!'

The grown-ups giggle and tease me:

'So Fahim, did you understand?'

I shrug. Serge, the group's other trainer, comes to my rescue:

'I'll explain, Fahim. Let's see, what do you like best?'

'Er, apricots?'

The grown-ups laugh so much they nearly fall off their chairs.

'Well, *une épectase* is a bit like if you were eating an apricot and choked on the stone.'

I honestly can't see what's so hilarious about choking to death on an apricot stone, but their laughter's catching. From then on, whenever the analysis of a move shows that one of the players is in an ideal position, everyone sighs: '*Ah, mais c'est l'épectase aux abricots!*'

'Xavier,' Hélène persists, 'next time could you please choose words that are more appropriate?'

The next day, Xavier arrives looking triumphant, with a clutch of words that are highly proper: 'bum-fuzzle', 'crapulous' and 'turdiform'. After that he tells me that I'm the lord of misrule: a case of the pot calling the kettle black, or as we would say in Bangladesh, of the sieve telling the needle it has a hole in it.

XP: *The French championship requires a huge amount of preparation, intense effort and immense concentration. Right from the start, Fahim seemed more interested in having fun, messing around and making friends, perfectly normal preoccupations for a naturally sociable child, but taken to extremes by him that year. He simply wasn't 'psyched up'.*

Every morning I would make him come to the apartment where I was staying, a quiet space for working away from the group. I would tell him about the player he was facing that day, show him his earlier games, explain his strengths and weaknesses. When Fahim came back from the tournament in the evening, he would input his moves into the computer and we would analyse them together.

I had been aware for a while that Fahim's openings

were weak. Because they offered no immediate gains he found them boring, and he would veer between a slightly lacklustre approach and flashes of brilliance that were intended to knock his opponent off kilter, while forgetting to prepare the ground for his next moves. He would come to his senses in the middle of the game, by which time he would find himself on the brink of disaster and left with no alternative but to salvage what he could. I had worked hard with him on his repertoire of openings, trying to get him to give up his preference for the Sicilian Dragon, a strong but risky opening that he loved. I'd taught him alternatives, especially the Classical Sicilian.

Just before the second round, I warned him:

'Fahim, the French championships attract not only the best players, but also the best trainers. They come here with their clubs and their "private stables".'

'Yeah, yeah. Can I go and play football?'

'No, listen to me! Every trainer knows the pet moves of the other players and their trainers. Every trainer prepares their protégés and equips them with secret weapons.'

Fahim shrugged, a gesture that had become a habit with him and that had a unique capacity to annoy me.

'You're a much better player than your opponent this afternoon, but he'll be making careful preparations. As we speak, he will undoubtedly be vetting every aspect of your game. When he comes to sit opposite you he will know you by heart. Look, he'll know already that you're far too fond of the Dragon.'

'OK.' He shrugged again.

'And his trainer specialises in countering bad variations of this opening. You absolutely have to play the Classical Sicilian.'

'OK. Now can I go and play football?'

He was miles away, elusive, impossible to pin down. He was crossing a minefield with a flower in the barrel of his gun. Predictably, he allowed his opponent to take him by surprise from the opening, and – prompted by a reflex reaction as much as nerves – he fell back on his Dragon. And he lost.

I tried to reassure myself that this setback was due simply to his lack of experience. This was his first national championship, whereas his opponents were tournament 'pros' who'd been coming since they were mere tots. I hoped that Fahim would quietly rise back up to the surface like a submarine, without alerting his opponents. But in his expression and his attitude I could detect a sadness, a level of anxiety that I'd never seen in him before.

I hardly ever call my father when I'm away. We don't need to speak to each other to be close. But that morning

I do decide to call him, and he tells me. That France has run out of money, that the Prefect is going to close down all places in emergency hostels, that 600 families are going to be put on the streets.

'Fahim,' he says, 'you absolutely have to win this championship. You're our last hope. If you win, "they" might take notice of us. This is the moment. You've got to get noticed. Do it for us. Don't come back without that trophy!'

XP: *With young players, parents hold in their hands the potential to do real harm. Some parents project their own ambitions on to their children and exert a terrible pressure on them, demanding the best results, the highest level, the most resounding victory. They fail to understand that all players play according to their individual abilities, progress at their own pace, and have to contend not only with that day's opponent but also with their own changing moods and fluctuations in concentration. They forget that in order to win you have to concentrate on the chessboard, not on the result, or else it's impossible to play well. How many times have I told my pupils:*

'Listen to the pieces, enter into the game, don't think about the result, stay receptive to whatever your position requires.'

And I'm not even talking here about parents who know nothing about chess, who see it solely in material terms and bemoan the loss of every piece, convinced that this is invariably due to some lapse in concentration, and blithely unaware that it might be the result of a strategic decision.

This was a problem I never had with Nura. He was perfectly capable of giving Fahim a dressing down if his attention wandered. But he never came to inveigle me with suggestions: 'You should tell him that ...' or 'He really needs to ...' One day, however, I'd made the mistake of remarking that if Fahim won the French championship it might help them to re-open their case. So when Nura heard that the emergency helpline for homeless people was going to be shut down, he put terrible pressure on Fahim. The more intense the tournament became, the less confidently Fahim seemed to play, and the less able he was to concentrate. His strokes of brilliance became increasingly rare. Several of my colleagues, having heard people sing the praises of this young champion who had come to scoop the title, were evidently deeply puzzled.

Despite all my tirades and pep talks, Fahim was indeed behaving like a submarine, but this was a submarine that had decided to sink down to the ocean floor and stay there. The result was a fiasco: Fahim finished in seventh place, behind players who were not only weaker than him but also less talented.

Coming on top of Fahim's lack of progress during the year, this defeat led me to do a lot of soul-searching. Where was the Fahim of our early days together, focused and headstrong, lively and determined? Had he been so damaged by the ordeals of life and his experiences in France that he was no longer capable of fulfilling his potential? Had his gifts vanished for ever? Or was it my fault: was I still the right trainer for him? Perhaps he needed a trainer who was younger, more like him?

Back in Paris, I asked one of my former pupils, Jonathan, if he would look after Fahim. Being young and of Indian origin, perhaps he could be more of a role model for Fahim? This looked as if it had a chance of working out, with the two of them planning practice sessions and tournaments. But Jonathan was busy and their plans got bogged down, and in the end I carried on as Fahim's trainer.

When I get back to Créteil, defeated and empty-handed, my father isn't even angry. He doesn't say anything. It's as though he isn't there. He doesn't say anything either when my school report arrives: my marks are in free fall and my start to the next school year is not exactly covered in glory.

At the beginning of the summer I play in the Paris championship again. Xavier pushes me to compete at the next level up:

'You don't play again for a title you've already won once.'

But I'm dead set on the idea of winning the 1,000 euro prize money, which we so desperately need, and I stay in the same category as last year. I finish in 47th place.

XP: *At the Paris championship another trainer came up to me looking rather smug:*

'Xavier, my pupil beat yours!'

'Yes, but just look at Fahim, take a good look at him. Do you have any idea why he lost? The emergency homeless service has just been closed down. The hostel where he and his father live has put them out on the street.'

July in Paris. It's part of my routine now. I call the emergency helpline. Every time my father's worried, on edge. Every time they say we can stay at the hostel for another fortnight. Until the day when the bomb drops:

'You have to vacate the room,' the lady says.

My heart misses a beat. I can't speak.

'Hello?'

'But where are we going to sleep?'

The lady is embarrassed:

'I don't know. I understand your difficulty, but we aren't allowed to give out rooms any more.'

I can't believe it. I hang up, then call back again straight away. Several times. It's the same answer every time. We're out on the street. It's all over. My luck has run out.

My father rushes off to see the social worker. Her name is Véronique, she's nice, she'll find a solution for us. But Véronique has gone, and the lady who's replaced her is chilly, indifferent, rude. As soon as we start to explain why we're there she throws us out. My father talks about her to this day:

'She very very not good.'

Of all the people we've met on our journey, I think she's the only one he bears a grudge against. While my father stays in Créteil to try to find a solution, Xavier takes me off to Marie-Jeanne's house for the summer. I spend my days daydreaming. I dream that I live on a boat, that I'm sailing around the world, that I explore everywhere and see everything. I dream I'm the most powerful man in the world, a lord, a king, an emperor. I dream of escaping this world, of walking on the clouds, of living on the moon. And when I come down to earth and realise that all this is impossible, I dream of simply being rich enough to buy a beautiful sports car and go wherever I want to. Especially to the European championships.

Back in Créteil, my father is living at the chess club, where Hélène has said we can stay for the summer. He sleeps on the sofa, but he'll have to leave when the new school year begins and the club starts up again. On the telephone he tells me all the things he's tried. He agreed with the president of a Paris chess club that in return for accommodation and pay he would clean their premises and teach for a few hours a week. The president painted a glowing picture of the advantages for me of going to school in a part of Paris that attracts the right sort of people and with a major high school close by. My father accepted on condition that I could continue to train at the Créteil club. My progress in chess mattered to him more than anything, and my trainer was Xavier! The president agreed, but then things got confused. The president announced online that I was joining his club, trying to put pressure on my father, who wouldn't give an inch. Then he dropped my father like a stone and gave him a tent instead.

When the Créteil club re-opens at the end of the August, my father goes off to live in his tent. He wants to pitch it in the grounds of the apartment building where the club has its premises, as this would be practical, but Hélène has to explain to him that it's not allowed. So he takes himself off and pitches it on the roof of a super-market, where no one can see him, and when he gets moved on from there he camps out beside a tennis court in some public gardens.

This is where I find him when I get back from Brittany at the end of the summer. The first night is awful. The ground is hard, a thunderstorm is rumbling and it starts to rain. My teeth are chattering, I'm cold and frightened, and I feel dirty and ashamed. All night I ask myself what I've done to fall so low. By the morning I'm in pieces. Devastated and lost for words, my father cannot bring himself to look at me.

XP: *The economic crisis that engulfed Europe in the late summer of 2011 brought with it a social crisis that was just as acute: long queues formed outside the 'Restos du Cœur' soup kitchens and food banks, and the shanty towns that had disappeared 50 years earlier from the verges of French motorways and the Paris ring-road sprang up once more. 'It's like the Tex Avery cartoon where everyone keeps passing round the stick of dynamite before it blows up,'*

lamented Xavier Emmanuelli, founder and president since 1993 of the Samu Social, which ran the homeless helpline, in his dramatic resignation speech. If even Emmanuelli had given up …

By that time I'd been feeling out of my depth for a while, unable to help Fahim and Nura. I had no more solutions to suggest, no more plans to offer: I'd run out of steam. And once they were out on the street I was unaware of their plight, as I was being chased by my publisher and had cut myself off from the world, physically and mentally, so as to devote my time to writing a long-promised book.

Paradoxically, my absence turned out to be a good thing. Fahim and Nura's plight had plunged the club into turmoil. That same evening, Hélène made calls to a number of families. Since the state had washed its hands of them and would no longer provide support services or any other humanitarian aid, ordinary citizens would have to roll up their sleeves. In my absence, the more caring, generous and open-minded members of the club took over. It's not hard to imagine the discussions that must have taken place in different homes that night:

'We can't let that boy sleep on the streets.'

'But we haven't got room to put him up.'

'We can make room. But we have to recognise that the delicate balance of family life is a fragile thing, and the arrival of an outsider can be challenging.'

'Yes, I know that, but if he dies of cold how can we ever look each other in the eye again?'

'You're right, we have to make room for him. But what about Nura? We can't separate them.'

'No, of course we can't, but we really haven't got enough room for two people. Let's take in Fahim, get him ready for the start of the school year and then take things one step at a time.'

'What will we do when we go away at weekends?'

'We haven't got all the answers right now. Let's start with tomorrow night. If we start the ball rolling other people might follow our example.'

With two children of her own, Anna-Gaëlle had room in her heart for more. She and her husband David were the first to open up their home to Fahim. Later on, Gilles – a loud, larger-than-life character with a pronounced Mediterranean twang – and his wife Christine were to step into the breach.

Every morning Anna-Gaëlle wakes me up – with difficulty – and I go to school. In the afternoon I go and find my father at the club. If he has any money he buys me a snack. Then I do my homework and work on my chess. The club office has become my study. In the evening we eat there, then my father walks me back to the apartment block where Anna-Gaëlle and David live. If they're still eating when I arrive, I sit down with them to eat some more. Then Anna-Gaëlle puts her sons to bed. I sit on the bed to listen to the bedtime stories she reads to them. When she stops reading I get up to go, but I pause in the doorway to watch as she kisses her children goodnight.

Then I go to bed and think. I think about my father on his way to the vast artificial lake in the middle of Créteil; my father waiting until it's dark, until the last fishermen and lovers have gone, before pitching his tent; choosing a spot where he won't get soaked at dawn by the automatic watering system; sleeping on a second-hand mattress, until it gets soaked by the rain and becomes unusable, and he has to sleep on the ground.

I think about my father zipping up his tent and taking one last look at the Préfecture building on the far side of the lake, orange in the daytime but gloomy at night, the same Préfecture that won't give us our papers. My father crying himself to sleep, wondering how it can be that a country as big as France, with so many buildings, can't find room for him, just a little space, so that he wouldn't have to sleep outside; my father praying, though he's not very religious, and asking his god angrily why he has abandoned him on the streets.

I think about my father getting up at dawn, opening his tent and looking out at the Préfecture, his first sight of the day, then rolling up the tent and heading off for the club, washing in the little handbasin (except on days when he has €1.50 and can go to the public baths at Châtelet); my father doing our laundry in the washbasin (except on days when he has €2.00 for the launderette) and draping it over the radiators to dry, on condition that he takes it off again before the club opens.

I think about my father getting provisions from the Restos du Cœur food bank, tidying away our cases, boxes and bags so they aren't in anyone's way, doing the washing up, dusting the shelves, sweeping and washing the floors, doing everything he can so that he won't have to hear people complaining that the club has become 'just like a campsite' and that it 'smells of frying'.

I think about my father going to the Préfecture, going to see the lawyer, going to see the interpreter, going to see Frédéric, going to French lessons, greeting the children at the club; and after everyone has left, leafing through the books that are left lying around, dozing on the banquette, letting the endless days drift past as he waits for me to come back.

I think about my father with no money and no one left, living only for me. My father who can't afford a Métro ticket any more, who can't afford to buy me a pen, or a jumper. My father filled with shame, forced to beg for everything he needs.

I think about my father who can't take any more, who is sinking a little deeper every day, who loses his temper for no reason, and then can't even get angry; my father who never tells me off any more, who never shouts at me, who never smacks me, who never talks to me, who never speaks, who just waits, holding his head in his hands.

I think about my father who I don't live with any more, my father who I pass in the hallway as children go in and out; my father who I am getting further and further away from, or who is getting further and further away from me, I don't know any more. I think of him at night and I can't sleep.

I'm tired. I don't do my schoolwork. I start being cheeky. The teachers tell me off. My marks take a nose-dive. My chess playing has never been so bad.

XP: *Nura never complained, but he exuded despair. He had aged. Life had etched itself on his features. Being forced to do nothing, to be useless and to live in fear had destroyed him. He would spend hours just sitting or lying, not saying a word, not doing a thing, not moving, not looking at*

anyone any more. He was so damaged that I used to wonder if he would ever be capable of turning things around again, of getting back on top of things so that one day he could get a job and reintegrate into society. I was equally at a loss with Fahim who, driven by feelings of solidarity, of unconscious imitation or despair, more and more often went to sit with him and do nothing too.

My father never stops thinking about Spain. Spain was his original destination, and he regrets having stopped en route. He often says that if we'd carried on he would already have papers, a house and a job. He says that if France doesn't want us, he should carry on to Spain. Every time I persuade him to change his mind. I tell him to wait for the Préfecture's response, I explain that I don't want to leave, that I've got used to France, that I don't speak Spanish, that I don't want to leave my school, Xavier, the club, my friends, that we'd have to begin all over again.

Even when he's not talking about Spain, he's thinking about it so hard that you can see it in his face. Then, with no work, nowhere to live, no money, no papers, no future and no strength left, stuck in a dead end and with his family far away, my father decides to make a fresh start and head for Spain. On his own. Without me. He says he'll leave me at Créteil and try his luck somewhere else. He says that Anna-Gaëlle, Hélène and above all Xavier will look after me, that I will have a good life, that his life lies elsewhere, that he will come back and fetch me if he gets papers, a job, money. Maybe.

I don't say a word. I scream.

Back at Anna-Gaëlle and David's apartment I run and hide in the bedroom. Anna-Gaëlle sees me as I tear past: she can tell at a glance that something serious has happened and comes to find me straight away. I burst into tears. I cry like a baby. She asks me questions, does her best to make out my answers, tries to console me, assures me that we'll find an answer. It's no use. I've lost my mother, I'm going to lose my father. I'm alone in the world. I want to die.

That night, I dream that I go to the club. It's all in darkness, the windows are broken, and I can sense a presence hiding in the shadows: a giant wearing glasses who I know without really knowing who it is. He has a long knife and is going to stab me. When I try to run away, someone pushes me back inside. I wake up with a start. My heart's thumping, I feel sick, I'm so frightened that I don't dare move an inch.

In the morning, David is sitting at his computer in the living room. Terribly worried, he's been up all night trying to find a way for my father to stay in France. He's sent a thousand messages in bottles across the ocean of the web. He's a journalist, and he knows a lot about all this. For days he tries everything he can think of, networking and making contacts, sometimes filled with hope and then discouraged again. Eventually he makes contact online with Catherine and Patrick, who live in Paris. They have a big apartment and are willing to take my father in. It isn't the first time for them: they've offered people a place to stay before.

Anna-Gaëlle and David are stunned by their generosity, and my father hardly dares believe it's true. But it is! Two days later, he moves into 'his' room, a proper bedroom with a bed, a mattress, blankets and a wardrobe. What luxury! That very night, the first big chill of the autumn falls over Paris, and over all the people who are still sleeping out there on the streets.

Catherine and Patrick treat my father like a king. They trust him with a key to 'his' room and another to 'their' apartment. They tell him to help himself to anything in the fridge and invite him to share their meals: I'm not the only one who thinks he's too thin.

When I go to bed at Anna-Gaëlle's or Gilles' I feel better now, reassured. I know that I'll see my father the next day. I know he won't have left for Spain, that he won't have frozen to death in the night. I know he's safe inside, and I don't have to feel guilty any more about being in the warm. I can breathe again.

Every afternoon, my father catches the Métro to Créteil to meet me at the club. We spend the evening together and have supper, just the two of us: this is our time for us – even if some people complain about the cooking smells, even if we don't really know what to say to each other.

At the weekend, Catherine and Patrick sometimes take my father with them to the country, to a big house with a garden, an orchard and a kitchen garden. To thank them, he stacks wood, cuts the grass, tidies the flowerbeds and digs the soil, just like he used to at the barracks in Dhaka. In the holidays they invite me too. In the middle of February, when it's ten degrees below zero, they ask if I'd like to go horse riding. I don't want to disappoint them so I say yes, but I'm terrified. I get to ride a pony that's actually quite cool and I manage not to fall off. In the end it's fun. How strange life can be: yesterday sleeping on the streets, today going horse riding.

But nothing is sorted yet. My father still has no papers, no right to stay in France, no money, no future. We're still waiting for answers from the Préfecture, and the refusals keep coming. I can feel that he hasn't completely given up on Spain.

XP: *The plight of Fahim and Nura had caused such a stir in Créteil that it reached the ears of the mayor, Laurent Cathala, who went into action on their behalf. He supported every one of their applications at the Préfecture, writing lengthy letters stressing their willingness to integrate, Fahim's success at school and his achievements at chess.*

Thus he formed a link in the chain of solidarity that had been forged around them, as if to protect them from the fate that seemed to be closing in on them so relentlessly. It is impossible to do justice to the herculean efforts made by certain organisations that can never be praised too highly, by some social workers and by many supporters who remained nameless. Some gave material or financial aid, others offered psychological and moral support, and others again found the time to send an email to the right person at the right time, to call over and over again on jammed phone lines until they managed to get an appointment, to write a letter of protest or to collect signatures for a petition. It was an image of suburban life far removed from the one we normally see in the media.

Not to be outdone, the little world of chess lived up to the motto of the International Chess Federation, Gens Una Sumus, *meaning 'We are one family'. Championships in particular offered opportunities for meetings, discussions and sharing notes. Some of the players and their families had heard about Fahim's success, and about his father's commitment. An appeal launched during a tournament even resulted in the manager of a supermarket making Nura a formal job offer so that he could obtain a work permit. But yet again it all came to nothing. We were making no headway at all.*

Chapter 12

JUST A SINGLE PAWN

Right from the start of the season, Xavier is absolutely clear:

'For years Créteil has competed at the highest level nationally, but we haven't won the trophy for … oh, I don't know how many years, I hardly dare count!'

'Oh go on, Xavier, tell us.'

We titter a bit, but Xavier frowns:

'There's a time for everything: a time for making a joke of things, and a time for competing. And this time the competition will be stiff. You're playing in the "first division" now. If you'd rather be playing marbles I'm sure you can find somewhere to do that round here. If you stay here, you stay here to train and to win that trophy.'

Someone whispers a silly joke in my ear. It's my good friend Isma (Ismaël is his real name, or Ismaboul to us), who's half-Tunisian and is always clowning about. Also in this year's team are Loulou, who's very serious but still funny, Yovann, who's half Indian and seriously driven, and Tanguy, the intellectual of the group. Then there's Tarujan, a Sri Lankan who's always chilled, Quan Anh, a half-French half-Vietnamese geek, and Aymeric, who's – French, I think. And me of course.

XP: *In my 30 years as a trainer, both for local teams and*

for the French national team, I've coached countless pupils from all over the world. Taken together, the Créteil youth team were ten years ahead of their age group at school, and represented – counting dual nationalities – six or seven different countries. Brainpower knows no national boundaries.

There's a very clear link, by contrast, between money and success. How could Fahim possibly compete on equal terms with players whose parents were able to lavish funds on chess coaching, lessons, trainers, courses, trips abroad and competitions? Not to mention the gulf that lay between him and the little Ukrainian and Chinese players who, though no more talented than him, were the product of state training programmes? Harshly treated by life as he was, limited to a single trainer, prevented by his irregular status from competing at international level, unable to take part in most national competitions for lack of funds, it was a miracle that Fahim was still playing at all.

'Well, Cannes will beat us anyway,' someone says.

'Yeah, they're really good.'

'They're terrifying!'

Xavier stops us:

'If the Cannes team is your *bête noire*, work out how to beat your *bête noire*.'

'But that's impossible!'

'Nothing is impossible to a willing heart! You know Karpov and Kasparov, the Starsky and Hutch of chess? The first time they played each other was in the world championship final in 1984. On one side Karpov, world champion since 1975. Opposite him Kasparov, a mere youth, spirited, still developing as a player and with no experience of playing at that level. And wham! Kasparov was down 5-0. At that time, when one player had won six games the championship was stopped. So Kasparov was determined that he wouldn't lose another game: they would all be wins or draws. He wouldn't cede a single point. And he held out, one game after another, and fought his way back up: 5-1, 5-2, 5-3, and so on and on. The match dragged on for ever. After 48 games and five months, Karpov couldn't stand the psychological stress any longer, and the match ended without a winner.'

'But that's a cop out!'

'The spectre of that match and the way it ended haunted Karpov for the rest of his life. Whenever he played Kasparov after that, at crucial moments he would just completely lose it, and there can be little doubt why. He couldn't get it out of his mind that this was the snotty-nosed kid that he just couldn't beat a sixth time.'

'He must have felt really bad about it!'

'I'm telling you this story to make you think. Which

of these two mental attitudes will you adopt when you face Cannes? Will you be like Kasparov, 5-0 down to the unbeatable world champion but absolutely determined never to give up? Or like Karpov, the heavyweight who loses his grip when he sees his opponent as his *bête noire*? If you go in to face Cannes like losers, they'll wipe the floor with you. It's like every sport, it's crucially important to go in with the right mindset.'

I love Xavier's stories. And I make up my mind that this season my mindset will be as tough as steel. I am totally psyched up. And I promise that after every lesson I'll do my exercises. I swear it! Even though I put them off that week, and the next week, and the week after. Sometimes I make the others laugh by telling them that I want to show Xavier I've really understood what the verb 'to procrastinate' means. It's fun making them laugh. But I will knuckle down, I know I will. Soon.

'So let's work out a strategy for beating our *bête noire*,' Xavier goes on. 'Has anyone got any ideas?'

'Er ...'

'The secret in this sort of case is to hang on to the initiative. The player who has the initiative imposes his own rhythm on his opponent, who can only try to catch up and fight back.'

'How?'

'Well, it's quite simple really: put his king in check

175

to put him on the defensive; make your own choice of which pieces to take and which ones to lose; or force him to react by threatening him. In short: check, take, threaten!'

Check, take, threaten. That's exactly what I dream of doing. And not just in chess either.

My first opponent at Top Jeunes, the youth tournament, is pretty weak. A walkover. So I let my mind wander, I make careless moves – and within a quarter of an hour I've lost my queen without taking his. A scary wake-up call! I go crazy. I might as well throw in the towel now. I'm furious – with myself, with my opponent, with the whole world. I'm so angry it hurts. I could almost hit the boy opposite me.

'A great player never dies without attempting a final flourish,' Xavier would say.

So I throw myself back into the fight with a last desperate push. And I don't back down. I resist for three hours, three long hours, without my queen. No one would bet a single *taka* on me winning, or even squeezing a draw. But I wear my opponent down, surprise him, knock him off balance, exhaust him – until finally he cracks and makes a stupid mistake. I win the game. It's brilliant. I love it! I'm happy. What style! I get up with a big grin on my face. Then I look at Xavier. He's furious.

'This is not just about you, Fahim! By acting like that you put the whole team in jeopardy. You've pulled the rug out from under their feet. The others were counting on you to win and the team was ahead. But when I could see you were going to lose—'

I shrug.

'But I won!'

'Shush! When I could see you were going to lose, I had to push the others to get the points we were going to need. I forced the ones who could have gone to a draw to carry on playing. I couldn't let them off with only half a point. I had to make them try to win, to get a full point. So they had no choice but to take risks, and some of them lost. All because of you!'

'Yeah, well, it's not my fault.'

'On the contrary, Fahim, it *is* your fault. *You* might have won, but because of you the Créteil team has lost the first round!'

XP: *Fahim's playing that year was distinguished only by his poor standard. His sole success was coming second in the Île-de-France versus England tournament, winning a*

177

ticket to Disneyland as his prize. I tried to get a response from him, but he just couldn't get himself together. He'd stopped making progress. In fact he was going backwards, and I was afraid that at any moment he might give up altogether. I've seen it happen to so many young players who have had their heads turned and then crashed out. Fahim would arrive late for lessons and training sessions, refused to apply himself, wouldn't put his games online or study them, and regularly 'forgot' to do his exercises. He was apathetic, dragged his feet, answered everything I said with a shrug, and was cheeky in his attitude. I wasn't the only one who noticed it. His teachers at school complained that he talked and fidgeted in class, skimped his work and was casual to the point of rudeness. He was starting to come unstuck, if not in the standard of his work then at least in terms of his future prospects and his attitude. How could it have been otherwise?

I hate my life, it's horrible. I used to find a refuge in chess. That was a battlefield where I was the king. Even better than that, in fact: I was the one who commanded the king, who gave him his orders. I used to know I was in charge of the army and of the game. But for a while now the game has been slipping through my fingers, just like my life. I'm not the one who decides any more. I'm less important than the king, whose survival governs the game; less important than a rook, which can cross the board to checkmate; less important than a bishop or a knight, which can't even checkmate on their own. Perhaps I'm only a pawn. If I'm just a pawn, who will take orders from me? Who will take any notice of me at all?

Xavier's not happy, it's perfectly obvious:

'Fahim, where did that good, polite, respectful, motivated boy go, the one I met that morning in February 2009?'

I shrug. I don't know what to say. I don't have any memory of that boy. I can barely remember that time, when my father and I lived together, when we thought we would always have a roof over our heads, food on our plates and pride in our hearts. When I still had hope that I would see my mother again.

Now I feel alone. I feel in danger. I don't believe in anything, I'm not expecting anything, I'm not hoping for anything. Every day is an ordeal. I leave my feelings, hopes and fears outside, then I shut the door and double-lock it. I move forward blindly, always on the look-out for a laugh, just to pass the time.

Christmas 2011. Despite the way I'm behaving, Xavier is still kind to us. To celebrate the holiday, he puts together a Christmas lunch at the chess club, just for my father and me.

'Foie gras and microwave ready meals: a real feast in the circumstances,' he greets us with a chuckle. He tells jokes and even manages to make my father smile.

We're in the middle of eating when the phone rings. Xavier answers it, and all of a sudden his face falls.

XP: *For some time my mother had been suffering from chronic bronchitis. On Christmas Day disaster fell: rushed to accident and emergency, she was rapidly diagnosed with advanced lung cancer. She had only a few weeks to live, just time for us to say our farewells.*

From then on I spent as much time as I possibly could with her, sharing breakfast with her, playing cards, talking, laughing – and crying. I gave up chess in favour of Scrabble, playing it with almost as much enthusiasm as chess, especially on one occasion when, after beating me (a rare event), she got up and put the game away, just to tease me:

'I want to bow out victorious, so that's our last game!'

Fortunately it didn't take much to persuade her to carry on playing – and losing.

Xavier isn't there. He comes to lessons, but he doesn't look at me. He doesn't say anything. At first I think he's angry with me.

'Fahim, my mother's ill. Gravely ill.'

His eyes are red.

'She needs me just now. And I need her. I want to spend all my time with her. Do you understand?'

Oh yes, I understand! I put on my casual air, but for once I don't shrug.

XP: *I know that Fahim and Nura must have missed me a great deal during this time. I fitted lessons in when I could, dashing off to the hospital straight afterwards. I could only listen with half an ear, even to Nura.*

One lunchtime I stopped off to buy a bottle of champagne: when there's nothing left to celebrate, there's always champagne. My mobile started to vibrate:

'Exavier, it's Nura. I no money left.'

'Listen Nura, I'm on my way to the hospital. Then I have to give a lesson in Paris. I'm not free until nine o'clock.'

'Exavier, I no money. Is all gone. I need. Big problem. Tonight no good, no shop. Shop shut. Now shop. Need eat.'

I looked at the bottle I was about to pay for. Only a complete bastard would refuse. But a detour via Créteil would mean that I'd miss visiting time at the hospital, and I wouldn't see my mother that day.

'Nura, I can't come to you. You come to me. Catch the bus at the Pompadour intersection, and I'll wait for you at La Croix-de-Berny. La Croix-de-Berny. Do you understand?'

Of course Nura didn't know the bus, he didn't know the bus stop and he never turned up. Furious at having wasted precious time waiting for him, but also filled with remorse, I went off to the hospital. I don't think Nura and Fahim had anything to eat that night.

Another time, when I'd rushed from the hospital to give him his lesson, I found Fahim sprawled on the sofa. When he told me he hadn't done his work I was so angry I was shaking: I could have stayed with my mother for another hour! I went outside and lit a cigar to calm myself down. 'He's only a child, it's up to me to find a way to get him to work again,' I tried to reason with myself. But did Fahim care about chess any more?

Xavier has vanished from my life. He's melted away. I see him at the club, when he comes for lessons and for my training sessions. But he comes without his laugh, without his stories, without his expressions. Without his will to see me win. Even before he leaves again, I'm facing everything alone: the chessboard, my life, my future. I keep my thoughts from wandering to the European championships: is it just a dream too far for a boy from Bangladesh?

I don't kid myself: soon, at my present rate, I'll only be eligible for the Val-de-Marne championships.

I try to remember. How was it that I used to be able to command my pieces on the chessboard, to tell the king where to go, order the queen about, force the pawns to sacrifice themselves? How did I manage to take control of my own life, to go in the directions I decided, to try to live a life with no regrets?

Then slowly, gradually, almost without noticing, I start to get a grip again. Without my father who is still silent, without Xavier who is so far away inside his head, I set out on my journey again alone. I travel over the chessboard, looking for the path to follow.

If Xavier was here he'd say: 'A long journey begins with a single step.'

That's another quotation from someone Chinese. I let my mind wander, thinking back to those openings that I haven't worked at. I try to remember what Xavier told me:

'Since you like the Sicilian, you should find out about all the Sicilians. With black, it could become your home ground, where you feel most comfortable. But you need to know your ground. Remember that Anand–Kramnik game: e4 c5 Nf3 d6 d4 cxd4 Nd4 ...'

I jump:

'Oh, that reminds me of my terrible Dragon at Montluçon!'

'Precisely, and you should have used a different variant.'

Feverishly, I arrange the pieces on the chessboard to replay these moves. I experiment with them, relishing them. I try different ways and I start to play, quickly. I imagine what Xavier's reaction would be, which variant he would suggest next, and I carry on.

The next day I come back again. Without Xavier the club feels empty. I hang around for a while, then finally sit down and go back to my 'home ground'.

'Fahim, you know so many Sicilian variations, you could use the details of one to perfect another. Look at that Judit Polgar game: when white does this, what does black do? Watch out, don't deploy your knight. You have a strong square for your knight, all the black squares, two open files towards the king, two diagonals ... Hold on a minute! Judit Polgar was Hungarian, not Russian, but that's no reason for her to retreat!'

Sometimes I stop, feeling discouraged, but inside my head Xavier urges me on:

'That's good. Now get right up to the net, like in tennis!'

And sometimes he tells me off:

'So how are you going to carry on with this game? Remember the Japanese proverb: "It's too late to think about digging a well when you're thirsty."'

If he was here I'd shrug my shoulders.

'There isn't bad.'

Or what about here?

'No! Right square, wrong piece!'

Or here?

'That's good. You're making progress. You're beginning to understand that tactics are not an end in themselves, but rather they're the meat of the overall strategy.'

I carry on, then stop suddenly:

'Xavier, I can't remember how I got here, I couldn't do it again.'

He would say:

'When you visit a town, knowing what its monuments are isn't enough, you have to remember how to find them too. Otherwise you'll never see them. When you first arrive, you pick out a few landmarks, such as a square, a statue or a building. You memorise two or three routes, and then you explore. Gradually you discover shortcuts, you get to know the one-way streets, you make the space your own. It's the same in chess. You know a few moves, then you learn how to prepare them, to find the paths that lead to them.'

Then he'd add:

'Maybe one day you'll start to look at chess as you might look at a town, in order to see its beauty. I hope you'll reach that level, and that, like Alekhine, you'll discover that chess is not a game but an art.'

When I've had enough of studying, I pretend it's a video game. Xavier wouldn't like it, but since he's not here ... It's true that chess is more like real life than *Mario Bros.* You can't miss a move and try it again a hundred times and always end up in the same place. So I pretend that I'm the trainer of a team of chess pieces, like playing *FIFA* on Anna-Gaëlle's computer.

February 2012: time for the Île-de-France youth festival. I turn up at the hall on my own, but because I don't have enough money I can't enter the tournament. Fortunately the referee pays for me out of his own pocket. Maybe I still have a little bit of luck left in reserve.

The competitors here are playing for a chance to qualify for the French championships. I've already qualified, so I play in a parallel competition. As I'm top of my section,

I play the reigning champion for the title of champion of the Île-de-France. The good news is that it's a blitz game: I love blitz! The bad news is that my opponent worries me: every time I play him I lose. I'm his 'client'.

We start to play. Unusually for me, I'm tense. But he spends too much time thinking and soon he's running out of time. So he gets in a rush, plays too quickly, moves his queen forward prematurely and loses her. Now I have an extra queen and time on the clock. I can breathe again! At that moment he decides to shake my hand and resign. Perhaps I really do have some luck left. I am awarded the trophy and – a video camera! I can't find anyone who'll buy it from me.

Marie-Jeanne's funeral is on a Tuesday. I can't go because I'm at school. When I see Xavier the next day, I try to say something, but I don't know what to say to someone who will never see his mother again. Then life goes on, and Xavier focuses on my training: the French championships are coming up soon.

'Fahim, to prepare let's work on this game. Kasparov is black, Korchnoi is white.'

I study the board. Like this, perhaps? Oops, that's risky. I try another way. Just as bad.

'Slow down, Fahim! You're playing first and thinking afterwards.'

I shrug.

'I know, I could see that, but I risked it anyway because ...'

'Because you're a risk-taker!'

I smile.

'I take, you take, he takes, we take, they lose. Look: Kasparov, an attacking player like you, chose the safer option for this move and went for a less risky endgame.'

'But my move has more style! And maybe I'll manage to confuse white?'

'Yup, at a championship for morons you'd win no problem.'

'OK, but going for the safer option's rubbish. Much better to win in style!'

'Which is better, to have style or to be the best player in the world?'

I hesitate. Xavier pretends not to notice.

'So, a5 or e5?'

'a5!'

'Is that a guess? Or a bluff? Zorro rides again, is that it? Fahim, let me tell you something: the good thing about chess is that however badly or well you play, you can only ever lose one-nil. But if you want to win, it's time you got over this urge to show off, this need to take risks just for the thrill of pulling out all the stops at the last moment. Do you understand?'

I say nothing. I think. I don't know whether I could ever surrender a great move, a spectacular coup, a last-minute flourish in order to show how rational and 'safe' a player I am. I think I'll always want to go down fighting!

XP: *Fahim was still at the top of the pupils' rankings, but as time went on the peloton was closing in on him. And I wasn't satisfied. Is a trainer ever satisfied? They can never see the progress their pupils are making. They forget that progress comes in incremental stages, and that these become clear only in retrospect. It's like when you're hill-walking, and the top of the hill still seems so far away: it's only when you look back down into the valley that you realise how far you've come.*

'One last game before the championships. A Guljajev problem, white's move.'

'I can't see it.'

'Be creative! You're smart, you're a survivor.'

I think for a long time, then play in one go, avoiding Xavier's eye.

'You see, Fahim: sometimes just a single pawn can rout an opposing army.'

I get the feeling he isn't talking just about chess.

Chapter 13

ENDGAME

It's Saturday. I'm in the hall. The players are milling around, looking for their places, putting bottles of water on their tables, scanning the room for familiar faces. I go and sit at the first table. My game will be streamed online, with a slight delay to avoid any possibility of cheating: what with earpieces, mobiles and all the other gizmos available nowadays, the organisers are becoming paranoid. Above the general racket a voice announces:

'Welcome to the 2012 French national chess championships. Our thanks go to the city of Nîmes ...'

No one pays any attention.

'From the 4,000 participants in the regional rounds, 900 have been selected to be here today ...'

Where is my opponent?

'Now could I ask families, trainers and accompanying adults to please leave the competition area?'

People crowd back towards the exit or climb up the tiers of seats, where they sit down and straight away get out their binoculars, scanning the scrum below in search of the right table. The hall empties. Soon just the players and referees are left.

'Now here is today's referee.'

'Hello everyone. I'd like to remind you of the timing for today's event. You have an hour and a half, plus 30 seconds for each move. I should draw your attention to a new rule by which a draw by mutual consent is no longer allowed. The referee may be asked to grant a draw only if the same position has been repeated three times, if neither player has the pieces necessary for checkmate, or in case of a stalemate, when the player whose turn it is to move is not in check but cannot move without allowing his king to be taken, which is illegal. If you have a problem, please raise your hand and we'll come and see you. I wish you all good luck. Please shake hands with your opponent. Black to start the clock, white to play.'

Suddenly the room falls silent. I'm not nervous. I never am at the start of a game. It's when it's all going wrong, when I'm on the point of losing, that the fear kicks in. Now I'm calm right away, in control.

Round one. My opponent, who's ranked lower than me, starts to play. I don't know him. I watch him. He sits slumped with his elbow on the table, his head propped on his hand, still as a statue. I want to shake him. I get annoyed, and this means I let my guard slip. The game goes on for ever. I doze. He dozes. He knocks over his Coke. I get up, walk round the room and come back. I miss the chance to checkmate him in one. He wakes up and starts to struggle like a fly trapped in a glass of water.

I get up again, this time to get a drink. I come back to the table. He tries to make a comeback and I get worried. Phew! I regain the advantage. I take the chance to stretch my legs. By the time I come back I've cooked up a secret potion in six or seven moves, to a recipe that comes from Xavier. He doesn't see it coming, not a thing. He swallows it whole. When he realises what's happened it's already too late. Checkmate! We raise our hands. A referee comes over to record the result. The number of players at the tables around us is dropping. Some of the losers are calm as they leave. Others look fed up, but at this stage in the competition it's still too early for tears.

XP: *We'd arrived the day before after a long drive, from Paris to Nîmes with Fahim and Olivier on board, plus a detour of 150 kilometres to pick up Quentin. When we arrived, late in the evening, Fahim didn't miss the chance to get in a gentle dig:*

'You're even better than my father at getting lost!'

The following morning I was up early to be at the ringside. Slightly dazed, and exhausted by events in my personal life. My colleague Serge and I spent time with our pupils, who came to see us to discuss their game, to hear a little about the opponents they were about to meet, and to brush up on their strategies. That year I had a dozen children under my wing. For the duration of the tournament, I was no longer their trainer: the time for training was over. Now they were the mountaineers and I was their climbing partner, anchoring their ropes. All twelve of them.

By the time the children head off to the competition hall, it's already too late. I rarely go with them, preferring to take advantage of the peace and quiet to have some lunch and try to relax. I have to be on form and mentally fit and alert. I'll be up preparing for the next round late into the night, when I'll know who my pupils will be playing the next day.

By early afternoon I've kissed goodbye to all my good resolutions. Invariably I find myself glued to my computer screen and following the games on the top tables, especially Fahim's.

Sunday. Round two. I play Guillaume. We know each other a bit. He beat me at Top Jeunes by skewering my queen and king. I'm wired: I want revenge. Yesterday's spilt Coke is sticky underfoot. You can hear people coming by the rip-rip-rip noise their shoes make. It makes me want to laugh, but it's distracting too. Luckily Guillaume plays badly. I stay poker-faced and get my own back on him for his enfilade in our last game. His queen has no choice but to commit hara-kiri to save the king. And then I refuse to retreat: the Russians never retreat! Guillaume loses his grip and resigns after seventeen moves. He congratulates me very nicely. I'm happy. I've got my revenge.

XP: *When Fahim came to see me I congratulated him: it was a magnificent game. It would be published in a number of magazines, moreover. It showed that he was back in tune with the dynamic of the game. He was even happier when he found out that someone had cleared the field by knocking out his* bête noire, *the player whose 'client' he had become.*

I was still concerned, nonetheless. Lacking the means to rent his own accommodation with guaranteed peace and quiet, as some of the other players had done, Fahim was sharing in all the holiday atmosphere, carefree fun and high-spirited excitement of the Créteil team lodgings. Nothing could have been further removed from the studious, focused atmosphere that is indispensable to any athlete in competition. At any opportunity he would cast concentration to the winds again and lark around with the others, hard to pin down and always eager to get back to having fun. I was afraid he might spoil his chances by getting some childish prank into his head, and I was always keeping him on the alert: during pre-game preparation, during post-game analysis, all the time.

'There are two rounds today. I don't know who you'll be playing this afternoon, so I can't prepare you. Look out, Fahim! Don't wait for the game to jump up and hit you in the face before you start to attack. Focus before the game. Stay quiet in the car on the way there, don't dissipate your energies. Half an hour of quiet and calm, in the real world and inside your head. Then don't mess up your opening! Watch out! I can feel disaster looming!'

Sunday afternoon. Round three. My opponent seems nice, with a little round face, freckles, curly hair and a shy look about him. So shy that he never attacks. Maybe he's too scared of losing. I get off to a bad start. I'm not concentrating hard enough, and I play too quickly in the opening and make a terrible blunder: I lose a central pawn and the right to castle. I'm on my tenth move and I've ruined all my chances. What's left but to resign?

No! I refuse to lose, or even to draw! Burning to win, I put everything on the table. I plough straight ahead, risking everything. I check, I take, I threaten: the more of my pawns my opponent takes, the more aggressively

I play. He's too concerned with protecting his pieces (Xavier would quote Mikhail Tal: 'Chess is made up of three components: time, space and last of all material'), and especially with protecting his queen – he doesn't see my checkmate coming. His fear of losing is my salvation!

XP: *As always, I had set up a quiet space away from the rest of the group, for the sake of my pupils' concentration and my own peace of mind during this intense week. As the afternoon wore on, I began to get phone calls and texts: I've won, I've lost. Then the first players returned. Some of them were bursting to tell me all about it, to explain, to celebrate, or to get it all off their chests. Others had gone to let off steam and would come later. When Fahim arrived I gave him a shake:*

'*So, are you proud of yourself?*'

'*Well, … I came out of it OK!*'

'*Wait! Going into a competition hall isn't like going swimming! Concentrate! If you let your mind wander you'll never get anywhere. React, for heaven's sake!*'

Fahim carried on protesting:

'*But I won, all the same.*'

'*You tread on a mine and lose a leg, and you come and tell me that it's great because you got to the end by*

hopping! And then what? Walking on your hands? Fahim,
what matters is not the game, it's your attitude, it's the
championship.'

Monday. Round four. As soon as my opponent sits down
opposite me he's virtually lost already. You can feel he
doesn't believe he's going to win. He's used to losing to
me: he's my 'client'. For me it's a stress-free game, a free
point more or less. I look around us: one boy is tying one
of his laces, another's daydreaming, a third is making a
lot of noise getting a snack out of a plastic bag. I get up
to go to the toilet. I've got time, unlike once when I was
up against the clock and had to hold it in with all my
strength, which shot my concentration to pieces. I come
back. Two players are signalling to the referee, crossing
their index fingers to say their game is a draw. One boy
has his head in his hands, chewing his lip, slumped in
his chair, twisting his fingers and drumming his feet on
the floor. He lifts his arms, stretches, raises and lowers
his shoulders and then takes up his position again, head
in hands. The players around him can feel the tension
mounting. The ones who are walking around are drawn
to his table like a magnet. A crowd gathers. Everyone
looks intently at the board, as though trying to help him

out in his desperate attempts to untangle the threads of his problem. Everyone holds their breath. Then he moves a piece, and the tension subsides. Everyone goes back to their places.

XP: *As the tournament goes on, the pressure becomes more intense. The system pits the strongest players against each other at the end of the tournament, and schedules the most important games at the point where everyone is beginning to feel tired.*

Tuesday. I catch Fahim just as he's racing out to kick a ball about instead of applying himself. He wins round five, but I'm still vigilant:

'There are just two players who have won all their games: Chesterkine and you. Look out, Fahim, there's still a long way to go!'

Wednesday. Round six. I'm up against the winner of the French championship at Troyes. I don't bear him a grudge any more for stealing the title from me: it wasn't his fault I couldn't be there. And in any case I want to live my life with no regrets.

Chesterkine looks Asian and is tall and laid back. He lives on the other side of the world, on an island that belongs to France. He has the back-up of a major trainer, but the place where he lives is so remote that he trains on Skype. Everyone says it's a paradise on earth in the middle of the ocean: it's called Tahiti.

So here we are, face to face. I might not bear a stupid grudge against him any more, but I have no intention of letting him win the title this time around. I manoeuvre for hours without success. So does he. I try to force the exchanges towards an endgame in my favour. Oh no! Too late. Chesterkine forks in the middle of the exchange. I lose a bishop with nothing to compensate for it. It's hopeless. End of story. I can already see my life passing in front of my eyes. I can't even propose a draw. Not with the new rule in place.

Then all of a sudden I remember Budapest and that game with Diana, when I couldn't move despite being a piece up. Of course! That's it! I speed up the pace so as to confuse him, so that he doesn't have time to think about sacrificing his pieces. I block his position, I put pawns everywhere, I close, for him it's like coming up against the walls of a fortress. The game goes on and on. Ten moves. Twenty. Thirty. He plays cleanly, efficiently, but he's not a killer. Meanwhile I wheel and deal, weave in and out, fight hand to hand, nab him. People gather round to watch: they're curious, convinced I'm going to lose. But he's attached to his pieces. There's not much time left on the clock. The game is stuck. We're going round in circles. We're in 'perpetual pursuit', repeating the same moves three times. It's a draw. I emerge exhausted but relieved.

XP: *When Fahim arrived I didn't need to tell him off. Our eyes met, and one look was enough. He'd made a big mistake: he knew it, and he knew that I knew. But I had to admit that even on his knees Fahim was still a tough opponent. Over supper that night the tension gave way to satisfaction, and we all laughed about it. Curious like the rest of them, he tried to work out the meanings of the mystery words of the day – including 'palindrome' and 'aibohphobia' (or the palindromic fear of palindromes) – before we moved on to our usual party games.*

The children told me about an incident that had shocked them. On the way out of the competition hall, one of the fathers, incandescent with rage because his son had lost, had grabbed the boy by the collar and thrown him into the boot of his car, before roaring off at top speed. If the world of chess can be a cruel place, how much more cruel can families be?

Thursday. Round seven. I face Théo, my football-playing friend from Montluçon. Still just as nice, still just as addicted to sweets. Sure of myself, I play fast and lack precision, letting a few good moves slip past. On the brink of a draw, I finally get my head above water and find my way to a good finale. I keep one eye on Chesterkine's table: he's winning too.

When I emerge from the hall people congratulate me, but I know what's coming:

'You played too quickly,' Xavier will say. 'You put yourself in danger again. I've warned you from the start. I've told you that something serious would happen, and now that's three times that you've been on the brink of disaster. Focus!'

Yet he doesn't seem as cross as I expected him to be. He speaks quietly. I'm almost tempted to think ... But no, I mustn't – a good player doesn't think about what the outcome will be!

Friday. Round eight. My opponent is a boy from Monaco, who seems nice. I don't understand why people from Monaco are competing in the French national championships, but then you could also wonder why I am. I play fast. There's no way Xavier will know, because I'm on the second table, which isn't streamed on the internet. The other guy plays well, but there's nothing he can do against the steamroller I put in place.

'Very good game,' says Xavier finally. 'Efficient and energetic.'

On the first table, Chesterkine wins.

XP: *Fahim and Chesterkine dominated the tournament. Each with 7.5 out of 8 points, they were way out in front of the other players: the rest of the field was now trailing far behind and posed no threat to them. It was rare for two players to have such a high score, 7.5 points often being enough to make a champion. If the two of them finished the tournament neck and neck, the winner would be decided by a rapid game play-off. With his quick wits, his intuitive approach and his competitive instincts, Fahim would stand a good chance. But he still had to face the last hurdle. The final round was the deciding one. They were playing for the title. From experience, I knew that nerves would win out over technique: either one of the players might crack.*

Saturday. Round nine. I shake my opponent's hand and banish all thoughts from my head. Above all, I mustn't think about my father, about the European championships, even about Chesterkine, who's sitting at his table a short distance away. The game is a tough one. After an hour and a half it doesn't feel good. My opponent's queen is reigning supreme over the centre of the board, and with the support of a bishop she controls all the black squares, whereas I've only got one rotten old pawn in the middle. I put my head in my hands, I jiggle my legs, I get ready to move a piece and then decide against it. I've got a sinking feeling in the pit of my stomach. I'm a dead man!

I get up and wander around. I go over to have a look at Chesterkine's table and – big surprise! – he has one less piece: a testing position – impossible to recover from, even – for a player who is so keen on his material. So it's Chesterkine who's the dead man!

I think on my feet: if he's going to lose, I don't need to win my game. I only need to draw. I'd be better off not taking risks in order to win at any price. But I hesitate. Inside my head I can hear Xavier's voice:

'Fahim, get over your urge to bluff. Even Kasparov sometimes goes for the safe option!'

I really hesitate. I want so badly to try my chances. But my decision is made. I change my strategy. I'm not going to win this battle, but I'm going to win the war! The weight pressing down on my chest lifts instantly. The tension melts away and I go back to my table, feeling calmer. I return to the game unworried, focused, determined not to lose. Almost enjoying making things difficult for my opponent, I defend myself every inch of the way.

Chesterkine leaves the hall, looking upset. I save my skin: a draw. I get up slowly. Am I there? I check the results on the scoreboard. I can hardly believe it. I've done it! I've won the French championship! I can feel an imaginary plane ticket in my hand, the ticket that will take me to Prague for the European championships. Then all my other dreams will come true. Maybe my name is already being inscribed on the North Pole ...

I start to move towards the exit, as though carried in triumph by my victorious army, when suddenly I hear a voice behind me:

'With no visa he won't be able to travel. He'll never go to the European championships.'

Soaring in mid-flight, my dream stalls, shatters into a thousand pieces and falls to earth. Undocumented, 'illegal' ... I'm a king in hiding. My legs nearly give way under me: I'm a champion, and it's all for nothing!

Chapter 14

CASE BY CASE

XP: *I hadn't stopped all morning, rushing around tidying up the mobile home I'd been staying in, putting everything away, doing the housework …*

'I know you didn't win, Marie. Don't be downhearted. You played a magnificent tournament. You deserve your medal, even if you didn't win the title.'

… giving back the keys, making a few telephone calls to sort out problems that apparently couldn't wait until Monday …

'Yes, Quentin. Brilliant! I'm proud of you. It won't be long before you're a master.'

… damn, my credit card's blocked …

'Oh Loulou, it just isn't your year! Hang on in there, your time will come.'

… ouch, that's my back gone again, better fill up with petrol, can't use my credit card, damn …

I arrived at the hall just as Fahim was coming out. He was quite calm, expressionless. People have an image of the national chess champion as looking like a young Mozart, a bespectacled prodigy who's clearly top of the class. Nothing could have been more different from the appearance of this young boy in his threadbare tracksuit and trainers.

'I drew and Chesterkine lost.'

He spoke quietly and didn't smile, even when I congratulated him. Too much excitement, perhaps. He called his father. I didn't understand what they said to each other, but I couldn't mistake the contrast between Fahim's reserve and Nura's deafening delight. He was about to call everyone who mattered to him and announce:

'Fahim, world champion of France!'

As we waited for the closing and awards ceremony, my pupils came up to me one by one, to show me their game, seek congratulations or reassurance, share one last joke or simply say hello. Only Fahim remained silent.

I go up to receive the trophy like a robot. I'm just an illegal immigrant. When I mount the podium, people clap and I smile.

XP: *It was already late when Fahim, Quentin and I set off on the drive back. On the way, I began to relax. One more day and I'd be on holiday. When we stopped to eat I called my sister. At the other end of the line I could hear celebrations, chants of 'Fahim! Fahim! Fahim!'*

The significance of what had just happened suddenly dawned on me. In my career as a trainer I've coached many French champions, but Fahim was special, both for his unusual situation and for the efforts I had made on his behalf. All at once, the stress of the journey ebbed away and I was flooded with feelings of calm. I gave Fahim a broad smile – and came up against a blank wall. His expression was still impenetrable. Could this be his own way of digesting what had happened?

I try to cling on to everything that's going through my head:

'Xavier, will you tell me that story you promised me if I became French champion?'

'Of course, a promise is a promise. I tell this story to all my pupils who win the French championship, and only to them. You in particular will really like this one. In the 1930s, Alekhine ...'

I'm hardly listening.

XP: *We made a detour to drop off Quentin and stopped for the night. I thought back over Fahim's story. It would make a good novel. Before we set off again the following morning, I posted a message on Facebook: 'Wanted: ghost*

writer for story of Fahim, 11 years old, homeless, visa-less and a national champion.'

It was already late in the afternoon when we reached Créteil. I headed straight to our arranged meeting point with Nura, dropped off my young champion, congratulated him again, and dashed off to the polling station. It was the first round of the presidential elections, and no way was I going to miss out on casting my vote.

By the evening I was back at home. At last! I was on holiday! Peace and quiet for a whole week. Before going to sleep I had a quick look on Facebook – and was staggered to discover that my post had received hundreds of 'likes' and was going viral. Someone was suggesting starting an online petition. Someone else was re-blogging the story. Someone else again wanted to write an article about it. All of a sudden I realised the urgency of the situation. If we wanted to get people talking about Nura and Fahim, to get their voices heard, to get them granted visas to stay in France, now was the time to act. It was now or never.

Next day I got straight on to the Federation to warn them that they needed to be on the front line. I asked around for anyone who had contacts in the media. All kinds of people – friends and strangers, acquaintances of Fahim or simply fellow chess-players, seasoned activists and observers stirred into action by the day's events – were following my example.

'You'll get some rest when I'm dead,' my mother used to say to me last winter when I took her up her morning croissants. Not yet though, it would seem. I began with the best of the specialist press, along the way making contact with Diana, the charming English journalist who lived in Budapest and already knew Fahim. Then I networked, following up my own contacts, then contacts of contacts, exploring every possible avenue.

The first signs of interest were not long in coming. The Créteil correspondent of Le Parisien *came to interview Fahim for the local pages of the newspaper. The culture magazine* Les Inrockuptibles, *where Anna-Gaëlle's husband David worked, had the same idea, and published a front-page article with great photos. Things were starting to happen at last!*

I tell the journalists my story:

'I came to France in 2008. Afterwards I came to live in Créteil, and then I began training at the chess club. Then I went to school and played in tournaments. Then I entered the French championships. And I won.'

And:

'I like playing chess because ... it's a duel, a duel between two players. It's like a video game, but it's for real.'

Xavier has worked so hard to make it happen that I try to make an effort with my answers.

XP: *The article didn't appear in* Le Parisien. *Great news! The editor had raised an objection: 'This isn't a story for the local pages; this is heavyweight material, it deserves the full treatment: we'll give it a full page in the national edition and move the photograph.'*

Fahim readied himself for another interview, with good grace but with no enthusiasm. The media circus neither upset him nor interested him. He understood what we were aiming for but he remained unmoved, unruffled. Had the experience of victory been such an ego-boost that being fêted by the media paled into insignificance in comparison? Since his victory he had seemed so far away: smiling and good-natured, certainly, but devoid of all enthusiasm. It was as though he was expecting something more. But what?

I don't tell anyone that I've won the tournament. I don't like talking about myself at all, let alone my wins. At school, no one apart from a handful of good friends knows that I play chess. Once a teacher even said to me:

'You're good at figures and you've got a logical mind, I'm sure you'd like chess. I could teach you if you like?'

I changed the subject to avoid the question. If he only knew ...

Now I feel even less like talking than ever. When people congratulate me and I have to smile I get a lump in my throat. Not being able to go to the European championships hurts so much.

XP: *The article in* Le Parisien Dimanche *burst on the scene like a bolt of lightning in a clear sky. It unleashed a procession of journalists, and the media machine went into overdrive. Overnight, I became like Tex Avery's Coyote, looking carefully to left and right before gingerly stepping out to cross a road in the middle of the desert, only to be mown down by hundreds of vehicles. Now all of a sudden here I was, a full-time press officer.*

A stream of journalists, photographers and television cameras descends on the chess club. Xavier has absolute faith in it all. He's convinced that in the end it will 'force the technocrats to budge'. He must be hoping that the publicity will reach the ears of the Prefect of Créteil, who will instantly pull the necessary papers out of a hat, as if by magic. Everyone around me is excited, especially my friends at the chess club, who appear in the background as extras and can watch themselves on television in the evening.

Occasionally I get carried along by their enthusiasm. It's almost as though I'm a celebrity: people are interested in me, they stop me in the street to ask if it's really me. Even my teachers at school seem impressed. So I play along with it, smile and answer questions nicely. I know that people think I'm happy. Fortunate, even. No one knows that I'd rather be living in total obscurity, just a face in the crowds of Créteil like any other kid, and have a plane ticket in my pocket.

XP: *Fahim soon learned that he shouldn't be too quick with his answers, that some questions would crop up over and over again …*

'Who is your favourite player?'

'Alekhine.'

'Why?'

'Because he was an attacking player like me.'

… and that there were some questions that didn't need answers:

'So Fahim, what does this place represent for you?'

It was all he could do to keep a straight face:

'Er, a chess club?'

He understood that a shrug of the shoulders was never a good response, and that it was much better to show himself in his best light, smiling and unaffected. He metamorphosed into a young media professional. The story of his victory was related far and wide, appearing in the Bangladeshi and Indian press and on television in Qatar. Fahim seemed to have captured the world's imagination.

Media pressure was now becoming a game changer. Hélène got a call from the security branch of the French police wanting to know more about Nura and Fahim's situation. And lo and behold they were given an appointment at the Préfecture for the following week. With any luck their file wouldn't have gone missing this time.

Friday morning, two days before the second round of the presidential elections. I was woken up by a flood of texts. Quick, turn on the radio, listen to the France Inter *morning show. It's amazing, people were saying. I held my breath and clicked on the podcast.*

'Our guest this morning is the prime minister, François Fillon. On the France Inter *phone lines we have a call for him from Marion in Paris. Good morning Marion.'*

'Good morning Monsieur Fillon, good morning France Inter. *Yesterday France learned that our new national under-12 chess champion is a young Bangladeshi boy who with his father has been living here as an undocumented migrant since 2008. For this reason, he is unable to compete in international championships. I would like to ask M. Fillon what he thinks of this state of affairs and what he would do for young Fahim if M. Sarkozy is re-elected. Thank you.'*

A few seconds later the answer came that was to change Fahim's life for ever:

'There are two things to consider here. The first is the general rule that within the territory of the French Republic, no one should remain in an irregular situation. The second is that certain people have their situation regularised, notably because of their potential to make a contribution to our country. If this young man is a chess champion, clearly his case is deserving of the closest attention. So we won't wait for the presidential elections, we'll look at this today.'

There was scarcely time to ask the question this begged – what if he hadn't been a French national champion? – before my phone started to ring non-stop. Every journalist in the land wanted to come to the club. By midday Hélène rang to say:

'*Xavier, I've just had the prime minister's office on the phone ...*'

Friday afternoon. School's out and I'm fed up. Some of my friends poke fun at me. Since the television cameras came to film us all coming out of the school gates at the end of the day, the whole school knows. That day the kids created such mayhem that the camera operator had to wait for them all to go and then ask me to come out again.

I head off to the club. I'm going to meet Xavier and my father. I dawdle along the way: there's no reason to hurry. When I get there Xavier is by himself, and his eyes look a bit red. Like when his mother was ill, but with a smile. A big smile.

'Fahim, I need to talk to you.'

'OK.'

'Do you know what's happened today?'

'Um, no ...'

He sits me down on the sofa and he tells me. All of a sudden it hits me. I bury my head in my hands:

'You don't mean to say the prime minister of France is interested in me?'

The week passes as though in a dream. The waiting drags on for ever. It's unbearable. What if it really is just a dream? All around me people are running around getting papers together, doing all they can to build up a dossier that no one can challenge.

Friday, 11 May 2012. We're on our way to the Préfecture. I have a smile on my face and fear in my stomach. Beside me, my father's expression remains impossible to read. He's dreading that there may be yet more unexpected problems: questions, demands, more waiting, another lost file. He won't believe it until he's holding our papers in his hand.

Outside the sunshine building, a handful of journalists are already waiting. The police officers smile at us, and one of them comes over to shake our hands. The mayor of Créteil, Laurent Cathala, arrives and greets us warmly. A man wearing a suit and holding a walkie-talkie comes to meet us at the gate and shows us the way. Laurent Cathala comes with us. I want to believe that this time it really is going to be good news. In my pockets my fingers are crossed. An entrance foyer, doors, corridors, stairs. At last we get there. On the door it says: 'Director of Immigration and Integration'. I'm relieved: no tickets, no endless queues, instead there are two men waiting for us. We go in. I feel intimidated. They exchange a few words with the mayor, then they turn to my father. I look on the desk and my heart misses a beat.

'Monsieur, here is your visa. It authorises you to live and work in France. And for your son, here is a *laissez-passer* that will allow him to travel within the Schengen area and to return to France without hindrance.'

My father is already holding out his hand to touch the precious document that will open all doors for us, when the mayor turns to say a few words to him. Suddenly everything seems to be happening too quickly, I'm not sure I can take it all in. My father looks at me as if to ask what's going on, and I translate in a whisper:

'The mayor's office is going to give us somewhere to live. And they've found a job for you ...'

Outside, it's crazy. Friends, long-time supporters and a great crowd of journalists are waiting for us. People greet us and congratulate us, and we all congratulate each other. They ask me questions:

'Now I'll be able to live with my father, in our own home ...'

I smile, really smile, smile at last. I believe it. It's true. Inside my head a new day is dawning and a future is stretching ahead. A future that starts with the European championships in Prague and then stretches on way into the distance.

Yesterday I was just a faceless unknown, visa-less, homeless and stateless. I was a nobody.

Today I am champion of France, and I'm on the way to becoming a normal person again.

EPILOGUE

Fahim's story ends here, at the moment when everything changed so dramatically for him, and he and his father were able to lead a normal life once more. So it falls to me to relate what happened next.

Three days after he received his papers, Nura started work. Ten days later, he and Fahim moved into an apartment, which was furnished for them by the network of supporters that had grown up around them. In under a fortnight, they had won everything for which they had been fighting for nearly three and a half years. Their nightmare was over. What a turnaround in their fortunes! Has a French championship title ever brought its winner so much?

In the summer Fahim flew off to the European championships, where his results were not brilliant. Life is not a fairytale. But a year later, in 2013, he won the World School Chess Championship.

Father and son are now inseparable again. Nura gets up at dawn and arrives at work every morning with the punctuality of someone who recognises the full value of what he has been given. Even if he is unwell he refuses to take time off, as he doesn't want his co-workers to have to cover for him. It is impossible not to admire his tireless determination. On the first Sunday of every month he takes advantage of the lifting of entrance fees to visit the museums and galleries of Paris. But the ordeals of the last few years have left their mark on him. While his dignity has been restored to him, he still says little, and for him solitude has become a way of life. Exile is always a wrench of the most visceral kind.

Fahim, for his part, is still waiting to see his mother again. He struggles now to find the talent and spirit that were so much a part of him when he arrived in France. He still nurtures ambitions, certainly, as though determined to get his own back on fate, and he is resolved never again to be in a position of need. But in snatching his childhood from him, life has clipped his wings. Fear continues to distil its poison. At his age, it's no easy matter to wipe the slate clean of three and a half years of hell. Fahim has already endured more hardship and sorrow than most adults in his adopted country will ever know. He's no longer a king in hiding, but he's still a king in recovery.

Yet as I watch him living from day to day, one minute so withdrawn and the next so dazzling, I can see that deep inside he's still a king.

Sophie Le Callennec

ACKNOWLEDGEMENTS

Sophie would like to express her enormous gratitude to Xavier and Fahim for the trust that they have shown in her in asking her to write this story with them and about them, and also for overcoming their natural diffidence in order to tell it to her.

Xavier and Fahim would like to thank Sophie

- for listening, for respecting their feelings and their silences,
- for her flights of fancy, disagreements and vetos,
- for her complicity and giggles,
- for her journey of discovery of chess, her sometimes bizarre questions (yes, Sophie, it's checkmate!) and the good grace with which she put up with them poking fun at her chess-playing skills,
- for her depiction in words of the experiences of players and trainers,
- for this book, and for their mutual affection.

Xavier, Fahim and Sophie would like to thank all those without whose involvement this book would never have been possible:

- the players and organisers of tournaments, who answered Sophie's questions and allowed her free access to the competition halls during events,
- France Terre d'Asile, Réseau Éducation Sans Frontières and Hors la Rue for their testimonies,
- the protagonists in this story who took the time to tell their stories,
- Nura, who despite the barriers of language and natural diffidence returned at length to painful past experiences,
- Marion and Laura, who generously lent their mummy to this project and patiently waited for her to finish her work before she finally realised that there was nothing in the fridge.

Fahim would like to express his immense gratitude to everyone, whether close friends or anonymous strangers, who has supported him and his father over the years, and who has made this story's happy ending possible. It's impossible for him to thank them all individually, but he would especially like to thank:

- Hélène, Anna-Gaëlle and David, Gilles and Marie-Christine, Catherine and Patrick,

- Muhamad, Frédéric and the CADA at Créteil,
- Yolande, Jean-Michel and the École Monge at Créteil,
- Laurent Cathala and the Mairie of Créteil,
- Alain, Alexis, Nadir, Nicolas, Isabelle ...
- the staff and volunteers of the humanitarian organisations,
- Bastien, Hadrien, Jean Baptiste, Joachim, Laura, Olivier ... and all the journalists who helped to make the Préfecture change its mind,
- Marion, loyal *France Inter* listener, without whom nothing would have happened,
- and of course Xavier, chess master, trainer and companion, in this book as in life.

How many children will we leave to sleep on the streets tonight?